Exploring Houston
with Children

by

Elaine L. Galit

and

Vikk Simmons

Republic of Texas Press

Library of Congress Cataloging-in-Publication Data

Galit, Elaine L.
  Exploring Houston with children / Elaine L. Galit and Vikk Simmons.
    p. cm.
  Includes index.
  ISBN 1-55622-839-2
  1. Houston (Tex.)–Guidebooks. 2. Family recreation–Texas–
Houston–Guidebooks. 3. Children–Travel–Texas–Houston–Guidebooks.
I. Simmons, Vikk. II. Title.
F394.H83 G35   2001   2001019226
917.64'1411—dc21   CIP

Dedication

To my family, my children and grandchildren, who always kept the faith. For my girls: Heidi, Shari, Lauri, Staci, Demi, Amanda (Mandi), Marisa, and Brandi.

And my guys: Randy, Jay, and Doug.

May we continue to explore the world together.

...And for Ray, who would have been proud.

With love,
Elaine

*****

To my parents who supported me; my daughter and son-in-law, Karen and Dustin, Kortney and Dylan, my grandchildren, and my goddaughters, Whitney and Julie, who inspired me. To Heather, Karen, Betty, Deborah, John, the Borders Artist Way gang—you know who you are—, and my many writer friends who shared the ups and downs. To Radha Mohini, Michael Seidman, Tracy Farrell, Phyllis Root, and Eric Kimmel who continue to light the path, and to Ginnie and Elaine who made it possible.

...And for Jack, who urged me to begin the journey so many years ago.

Thank you,
Vikk

Contents

Chapter

1   Blast off into Space!

Chapter

2   Bugs, Bats, and Butterflies!

Chapter

3   Where Fun Has No Boundaries!

Chapter
4 Playgrounds of the Mind!

Chapter
5 Day Tripping!

Chapter

6 Magic Carpet Ride!

Chapter

7 Mr. Smith Goes to Washington!

Chapter
8 In Your Own Backyard!

Chapter
9 Where Fun is the only Game in Town!

Acknowledgments

This book would not exist without the generous assistance of a great many people—family, friends, and coworkers to name a few. Certainly our own grandchildren have served to keep us focused on our intention of finding ways to introduce Houston to kids in a fun, friendly, and educational way.

We would like to thank a number of people who took time out of their busy lives to help and guide us. Any errors, though, are ours and not theirs.

The book benefited enormously from the sound advice, tips, and suggestions from Diane Durbin, Gracie Greer, Cynthia Littwitz, Amy Mitamura, Norma Belkin, Felice Goff, and Kat Sommers. Thanks also to Mark Goodland for caring, Elaine Gladstone for her unending encouragement, and Roberta Jacobs, who helped complete the journey. We couldn't have finished the manuscript without Jennifer Zoch Selewach, who pitched in and helped whenever called. A special thank-you to our editor, Ginnie Bivona, who believed in us and our vision.

Finally, we are indebted to the following people who generously gave of their time and knowledge: Joy Sewing, Mindy O'Bannon and Shirley Caldwell of the Houston Parks and Recreation Department; Betty Henderson and Mary Ann Weber from Edith L. Moore Nature Sanctuary; the Galveston Historical Foundation's Lydia Miller; Moody Gardens' Kelly Drinnen, Lisa Samuel, and Heather Dubose; Houston Museum of Natural Science's Dr. Carolyn Sumners, Laurel Ladwig, J.B. Howell, Betty Glass, and Barbara Wilson; Space Center Houston and JSC Educator Resource Center's Cynthia McArthur, Angela Case, Michelle Eckles, and Bobbie Sellers, Laurie Murphy, and Norm Chaffee; and Galveston Island's Convention & Visitors Bureau's Christine Hopkins, and Lorene Nieto.

Why We Wrote This Book

The world is full of playgrounds, playgrounds of the imagination. Museums, aquariums, and nature habitats all serve as educational resources, but to a child they are more. They are playgrounds that engage children's senses and bring them more fully into the world around them. *Exploring Houston with Children* not only provides information about some of the vast and wonderful sights the city has to offer, but also furnishes tips, techniques, and strategies that enrich the child's experience.

We hope this book will be more than a travel guide to fun places in the city of Houston. We hope it will become a resource for places that provide entertainment and enjoyment for kids while enhancing their education. Parents, home schoolers, teachers, and community leaders will find this an interesting and instructive guide to the city of Houston and its surrounding area.

How to Use This Guide

Children are born curious. They ask why. They ask how. They ask who, what, when, and where. The best thing you can do for any child is to create a rich learning environment. One way is to stimulate their curiosity by showing them that the world is a fascinating place and then helping them to explore it. Our purpose in developing this guide is not only to showcase places in the Houston area that provide entertainment for kids, but also to enhance their education by making these excursions more like fun family field trips.

Does this mean you need a special degree in education or must spend a lot of money? No. It does mean that you can help any child grow up with interesting things to do. It means you can help expose children to diverse and varied experiences. Fascinating places exist even in your own backyard, and Houston is full of places to explore.

We've taken the concept of school field trips and given it a fresh twist. Instead of simply listing a variety of places to go and things to see in the Houston area, we've gone a step further and provided tips and suggestions we hope will make the experiences more enjoyable as well as more educational. There are suggestions to help you prepare for the field trip, tips to make the visits easier, and activities and resources—including lists of related web sites—to help you reinforce the impact of the field trip. Our goal is to help you explore Houston and nearby areas and provide a sort of toolbox containing a variety of suggestions that will stimulate curiosity and aid you in answering those all-important five Ws: who, what, when, where, and why.

Think of our guide as an ally, a friend, but don't stop with what we say. Use our suggestions and resources as springboards for your own explorations and to create your own field trips. After all, you're never too young, too old, or too curious. Now, go out and explore the city!

Tips:

Some necessary items to bring with you:

- Snacks
- Map
- Tissues and/or wipes
- Quarters
- Toys, books, and games
- Tapes/CDs
- First aid kit
- Jacket
- Sunscreen
- Insect repellant
- Camera, film, batteries
- Notebook, pencils, and crayons
- But most of all, don't forget your sense of humor!

Other suggestions:

- Dress all the kids in matching outfits, the same color hat or other clothing item. That way they'll be easier to spot in a crowd.
- Take a movie camera or tape recorder to get reactions, comments, etc.
- Be aware of their expectations and be prepared for the unexpected.
- Have an alternate rainy day option.
- Make the children a plan not a promise. That way they will be able to accept, "we can't go because it's raining."

Disclaimer:

Please: be aware that although the facts recorded in this book are accurate and current as of this date, note that:

- Hours change

- Exhibits rotate
- Admission prices can increase
- Places close either temporarily or permanently so…
  Always call before going to attractions!

Key to Using This Guide

The concept is simple: learning is fun. Rather than do one more book listing places to go in Houston, we looked with a fresh eye and targeted the educational aspects of a wide variety of places in Houston and have grouped them accordingly. Be aware that many—if not most—of the facilities are multidisciplined in the application of the core curriculum, but we have singled out what we thought was the major focus. The breakdown is as follows:

- *Blast into Space!* is strong in astronomy, physics, and the hard sciences.

- *Bugs, Bats, and Butterflies!* hits the life sciences hard, including environmental science.

- *Where Fun Has No Boundaries!* is all about recreation, pure and simple, and leans toward physical fitness and sports with nature and biology a close second.

- *Playgrounds of the Mind!* is essentially museums that are kid friendly. The subjects include the performing arts as well as other disciplines.

- *Day Tripping!* is a bit of a mixed bag. While heavy in history, it does make room for conservation and biology. These diverse subjects appear under this heading because you could easily spend a day visiting each site.

- *Magic Carpet Ride!* focuses on cultural studies in history and geography.

- *Mr. Smith Goes to Washington!* deals primarily with civics along with economics and law enforcement.

- *In Your Own Backyard!* brings the curriculum home with a variety of activities and suggested explorations.
- *Where Fun is the Only Game in Town!*, as it suggests, focuses on fun and lists several major amusement parks.

After a brief introduction, five to seven facilities are featured in depth and more are listed in each chapter. In addition, we've added a *Toolbox* and *Resources* that provide suggested activities and lists of books, magazines, and web sites in order to expand the learning experiences of the child. Our hope is that we will make it a little easier for parents, educators, and community leaders to encourage and stimulate the child's curiosity in these subjects and pave the way for lifelong passions.

While we definitely think these extracurriculars are important and can easily be used to enhance the child's learning experience, we know that in this hectic, modern age time is a valuable commodity. For that reason alone it makes sense to have these visits as richly enhanced as possible, and we also know when parents become involved in their children's learning, the children do better. To that end, we strove to provide as many jump-starters as we could so that excitement and interest are fostered *before* their visit and maintained during and after.

Finding an appropriate blend of education and recreation for children is about as easy as parents trying to juggle the demands of work and family. So it becomes essential to set priorities and to remember to leave some down time for the child. Children need to study, but they also need the freedom to run and play. What they don't need are uninterrupted hours on the computer or nonstop time on the electronic games. There are many places in Houston that can provide a stimulating environment, which, in turn, could foster a lifelong love of learning. But the real nurturing comes from the adults: the parents, mentors, and teachers who in their attitude and excitement encourage the natural wonder of a child. Be willing to help them answer the who-what-when-where-and-why.

* * *

A Note to Parents—When we began work on this project we had no idea of the depth and breadth of the educational opportunities that are available. There are so many ways to have fun and learn at the same time. If you have birthdays coming up, consider having a simulated Mars Mission as the framework for the party at one of the Challenger Learning Centers, or maybe plan an exotic rain-forest celebration at Moody Gardens Rainforest Pyramid. The Edith L. Moore Habitat offers fun-filled nature birthday parties for a nominal fee. Instead of mountains of toys, consider giving your child or grandchild an experience to remember.

A Note to Home Schoolers—We were amazed at the opportunities that exist for parents, teachers, and home schoolers. Most places do accept home school groups for their school education programs, and many are willing to modify their programs to answer your needs. Ask. Also, we found home school educators are welcome to attend most educator-based workshops and learning experiences. Again, ask. We have incorporated some of the educator opportunities.

A Note to Educators—This is definitely the age of school programs. We have included the details of a number of school-based programs throughout the book. We sought out kid-friendly, education-oriented facilities and talked to the education departments about their programs. We tried to include as much information as possible to give our readers a sense of what is going on in Houston. All of the program directors we spoke to were quite willing to work with teachers and schools to ensure classroom needs are met.

A Note to Community Leaders—Many facilities have developed programs that meet the requirements of certain Boy Scout and Girl Scout badges and offer special programs and specific days when they occur. We noted a great amount of flexibility on the part of the education departments and definite interest in meeting the community's needs.

Opening the Toolbox

Each of the first seven chapters has its own *Toolbox*. This is where you go once a decision has been made to visit one of the facilities we've listed. The tools are activities that complement the subject matter of the various facilities featured. We hope they will serve as springboards for your creativity in finding ways to prepare, enjoy, and enhance the learning experience. You will find further activities in the *Backpack* section. These activities work across the curriculum and have a broad range; they are easily adapted to the disciplines. Rather than repeating those exercises in every chapter, we have given them their own.

Other Listings

Following each chapter's featured sites, we have included a less-detailed summary of other places. Although the educational aspects are covered, we did not go into any great detail on the education programs offered or provide any activities or exercises. However, with a little creativity you can reframe most of the exercises to fit these facilities, too. And, of course, you may simply create your own.

Using the Related Resources

At the end of each chapter, we have provided a list of books and web sites that relate either to the topic of the featured facilities or to the curriculum outlined earlier. Again, these are provided to give you and the kids some place to start when you prepare for the visit and afterwards to reinforce both the experience and knowledge gained. Most web sites listed have related subject links on their sites, making it easy for you or your child to pursue the subject matter. All sites were working when this book went to print; however, it is possible that some may have changed.

The Value of Docents

Many of the facilities mentioned in this book have docents who are there to assist you, to answer your questions, to make your trip easier and more enjoyable. These people have volunteered their time and undergone training in order to help visitors.

They are there because they have an interest in the subject matter, and they want to provide help and offer their services. Docents want to share their passion because they enjoy what they're doing. Don't be shy. They can share stories, open a window into a new world, then invite you into the world they've chosen to study. Let them help ignite a new interest in your child.

The Backpack

The *Backpack* holds activities and exercises that can easily be adapted for any discipline being studied, as well as some suggestions. Most deal with Language Arts and provide ways to enhance the visit and preserve the memory. Reading and writing serve as support columns for all learning. These activities are tried and true, and we have included them to help children capture and re-experience their visits.

Looking with a New Eye

Our senses are assaulted every day, and over time we tend to mask ourselves and withdraw from our everyday lives. Too often city dwellers do not "see" their own city. Do the following exercises with your child. Try looking with a fresh eye:

Houston as a vacation city

Instead of leaving town for a vacation, why not stay home and adopt "tourist eyes?" Many times native city dwellers do not even go to the celebrated sites. Pretend you're a tourist and look at the city with new eyes. Children, born with a sense of wonder, gradually lose their ability to see their environment. Slow down and really take time to look at your surroundings. You can experience this wonder with children in your own backyard. Pick a specific area, and both you and your child take a hard look at the environment around you. Don't do this part together. Write down some of the details you notice. Then have your child do the same thing. Compare your observations. Who had the true sight?

Is it round or is it lumpy?

This exercise is all about discernment and seeing the particular. Obtain some oranges. Then, place each orange on a counter or table. Use a journal or piece of paper and write down what you see. The orange has a universal shape. It is one color. What else do you see? The same thing everyone else sees? This is seeing the universal. Now pick up the oranges and take a long look. Examine every inch of the orange. Note your observations. Is the orange still round, smooth, and orange? Compare your answers. You should now have seen the specifics. This is the first lesson in observation, a needed skill for children to acquire. Try doing the same thing with different objects.

The Art of Journal Writing

Journaling has been a tool for scientists and writers over the centuries. It can be applied to almost any situation in one form or another. When used in keeping a personal journal, the writing is often reflective. When used in maintaining a scientific logbook, it has a more active role. The skill of observation is magnified when a person uses a journal. She slows down, observes, and connects with her environment. Keeping a journal can help a child hold onto a more vivid memory.

The Nature Journal

Journals are trade tools for explorers and naturalists. The act of capturing what you see, hear, and feel develops observation skills. Pick a fairly large plot of land where you can go and observe every day. Often nature journals have as many sketches as they have written entries. Note the date, time, the weather, and anything else you might observe. Sit quietly and wait. Capture the sights and sounds, the feel, the texture of the place. Sketch what you see, maybe draw a map of the selected area. Visit the spot at different times of day and record your observations: weather, trees, plant species, any evidence of animals and activity. Sometimes children are uncomfortable keeping a journal in the beginning, but if they see an adult keeping one, they will usually mimic and keep their own. Do this for a week, a month, or a season. Over time the subtle changes will become evident.

Kortney and Dylan make notes about their discoveries. © Vikk Simmons, 2001.

The Shared Journal

Sharing a journal with someone makes for an interesting exercise. Sometimes entire families participate and write their own reflections of holidays and special events. Don't be surprised if it brings the journal partners closer. Using a journal to record your adventures while discovering nature with your child can be rewarding since kids are so full of wonder and surprise. Decide what type of entries you want and how often.

Scrapbooks & Photographs

Photographs are a great way to record events and capture the experience. Children love to take photographs of what they do so they can remember and share the moment with their friends. The child becomes very involved in the whole process.

There are many types of cameras available that are suitable for children. Often the disposable types are used on trips. Be sure to spend time teaching the child how to frame a photograph so they don't have a bunch of headless, footless people in the photographs.

Picking out the journal book is a fun thing for a child to do. There are many styles and kinds. Stickers are an added extra. What child doesn't like to have his arms, face, and hands covered in bright, bold stickers? A decorated scrapbook page with photographs and stickers fascinates children. Writing the photograph captions can be a lot of fun. Sometimes the pictures tell a story. As an exercise, encourage the child to find a story within a group of photographs and then make a story scrapbook. Postcards are another favorite stimulus—and one that is inexpensive.

The Art of the Story

Children love stories. They love to hear them; they love to tell them. Here are some suggestions to get you started:

- After a visit to the zoo, a nature center, or a habitat, have the child write a story about what he saw.

- After a visit to the San Jacinto Battlefield, ask the child to imagine what it would be like if he or she had witnessed the battle or even participated. What would they have done?

- After a visit to the observatory or the planetarium, ask the child what it would be like to live on Mars. What would a person need? How would living on Mars be any different from living on Earth?

The Importance of Reading and of Visiting Libraries

Libraries have undergone many changes over the last five to ten years due to all the technological advancements. Now you can do a *search* for the books you're interested in, using your home computer. You can even put books on hold and renew them from your home.

Reading is important to the development of every person, adult or child. Reading is also something that can enhance the visits both before and after. Biographies abound. Have your child read them. There are also many web sites linked to the lives of great people: scientists, explorers, athletes, and world leaders. There are wonderful children's books published every year; so many choices exist for your child to read as follow-up to a visit. Encourage them to know more, to turn to books and read the real-life adventures.

Be sure your child has a library card of his or her own. You might even consider taking the child for a visit to the large downtown Houston library. Before you go, visit the library's web site and check out the "Kid's Page." There are *Hot Sites*, *Homework Sites*, and search engines. Hot sites range from the Ancient Olympics to the official Pokemon web site. Houston has a wealth of libraries; here are a few:

Houston Public Library (HPL) – www.hpl.lib.tx.us
HPL's Kid's Page – http://www.hpl.lib.tx.us/youth/kids/
Harris County Public Library – www.hcpl.net
Galveston County Library – www.rosenberg-library.org
Rice Library – www.rice.lib.me.us

The Internet has library resources, too. Try these:
Library of Congress Online – www.loc.gov
World Wide Library Directory – http://www.webpan.com/
msauers/libdir/index.html

Texas School Libraries – http://www.tea.state.tx.us/technology/libraries/

Be aware that, although the Internet contains a wealth of information, most of it accurate, there is also inaccurate information floating in cyberspace. Be sure to double check the source. While it's good to encourage your child to do further research using the computer, it's still a good idea for him to hit the books. Many teachers limit the number of Internet resources a child may include when writing her papers, and they insist books be included as references. However, if your child wants to pursue a subject and discover more, the Internet sites can be fun, colorful, informational, and interactive.

Children's Literature Links

Database of Award Winning Children's Literature (by Lisa R. Bartle)
http://www2.wcoil.com/~ellerbee/cgi-bin/childlit.html

Jan Brett's Homepage (beautiful)
http://www/janbrett/com/

Fairy Tales: Origins and Evolution
http://www.darkgoddess.com/fairy/index.htm

Ring of Fairy Tales, Folktales, and Mythology
http://www.darkgoddess.com/fairy/ftring.htm

Tellitagan Stories for Children (software for children)
http://www.tellitagan.com/ring.htm

Tomie dePaola
http://www.opendoor.com/bingley/mywebpage.html

*Once Upon a Time...*a children's literature web site by Dr. Mary Ellen Van Camp, Ball State University (This site is loaded with lots of stuff!)
http://nova.bsuvc.bsu.edu/~00mevancamp/ouat.html

Children's Book Council
http://www/cbcbooks.org/

Teachers at Random (Random House)—Teacher's guides to Random House books
http://www.randomhous.com/teachers/

International Reading Association—Children's Right to Read
http://www.reading.org/advocacy/makadiff.html

Texas Reading Club Manuals Cumulative Index 1986-1998
http://www.tsl.state.tx.us/ld/pubs/trcmanualindex/

Read Across America
http://www.nea.org/readacross/kidsbooks.html

Children's Authors by State (scholastic authors)
http://teacher.scholastic.com/authorsandbooks/authorvisit/list.htm

Texas Reading Club
http://www.tsl.state.tx.us/LD/ReadingClub/rcindex.html

Author Online! Aaron Shepard's Homepage—Storytelling and reader's theater
http://www.aaronshep.com/index.html#rt

The Story Place—The Children's Digital Library of the Public Library of Charlotte and Mecklenberg County
http://www.storyplace.org/storyplace.asp

Between the Lions—New PBS show for learning to read
http://www.pbs.org/wgbh/lions/

Suzy Red's Little Red Schoolhouse—Bluebonnet site, but much more
http://suzyred.home.texas.net/index.html

Children's Lit Web Links from Houston Public Library
http://www.hpl.lib.tx.us/youth/ncbw_links.html

Children's Illustrators
http://www.phylliscahill.com/greatsites/sites.html

Children's Book Council Online
   http://www.cbcbooks.org/

Seusville
   http://www.randomhouse.com/seussville/

Children's Book Council
   http://www.cbcbooks.org/navigation/teaindex.htm

Connecting Young Adults and Reading (Patrick Jones/District 8)
   http://www.connectingya.com/powering.ppt

The Children's Literature Web Guide
   http://www.acs.ucalgary.ca/~dkbrown/

ALA Resources for Parents, Teens, and Kids
   http://www.ala.org/parents/index.html

Connecting Young Adults and Books (Patrick Jones)
   www.connectingya.com

Reader's Advisory on the Internet
   http://www.fictional.org/ranetfull.html

Blast off into Space!

For many people the words Houston and space are synonymous. Say "NASA" and people think Mission Control in Houston. Astronomy, the branch of science that focuses on the skies, is big business in Houston. Every week Houstonians look up from the Earth into a vast array of planets and stars, asteroids and meteorites, and a whole host of other celestial bodies.

On Saturday nights volunteer amateur astronomers pack up their telescopes and go out to the Fort Bend Observatory for an informal star party. One volunteer mounts a camera onto his telescope and points out Apollo landing sites on the moon. Another uses his own invention, a "couch potato telescope" with a swiveling lawn chair and a pair of binoculars. Parents pack picnic dinners and mosquito repellent and go off to enjoy the natural beauty of Brazos Bend State Park while they wait for the night sky to appear.

The folks at the observatory say their job is "to get people to look up." Education, not astronomy, is their purpose. They are said to have the largest telescope open to the public on a regular basis west of the Mississippi River. Children see Saturn and babies eye Jupiter. Galaxies, asteroids, and the Milky Way are the talk of the evening.

We are fortunate to live in a city with such excellent space-related resources as Space Center Houston, the Fort Bend Observatory, the Burke Baker Planetarium, and not one, but two Challenger Learning Centers. Tram rides to NASA Johnson Space Center (JSC) from Space Center Houston are available and allow the public to take a peek behind the scenes. See Mission Control, the Space Shuttle Training Facility, the Space Environment Simulation Laboratory, and maybe even astronauts training for upcoming missions. The educational resources provided by NASA through the JSC Educational Center in the way of programs and material for the general public and for educators are overwhelming.

Do kids still like astronomy? Yes, but today it competes with many other activities for their time and attention. Does astronomy have relevance in today's culture? That depends. If we hope to gain a better sense of who we are, where we came from, where we are going, and even more important, where we *can* go, then the answer is yes. What skills should kids have? In a recent article in *Astronomy Magazine*, Marica Bartusiak says, "If you think knowledge of the night sky is a prerequisite for becoming an astronomer, think again. Math, physics, and computer skills are what you really need."

If your child is caught by the astro-bug, if he is fascinated with the night sky and telescopes, if she is curious by nature, make plans now to visit the following space facilities. Your child will find a window to the world of astronomy at the George Observatory in Brazos Park when he or she sees the moon through the 36" telescope, one of the largest in the country. Let your child experience the virtual reality of going to the moon or visiting Haley's comet through the Challenger Learning Centers, or come face to face with reality when they see the actual space station at NASA.

Don't stop there. Get on the Internet. Visit NASA web sites. Check out nationwide educational programs like *Project Astro* (www.aspsky.org/project_astro.html) and *Hands-On Universe* (http://hou.lbl.gov/). Contact local astronomy groups and find out when the next star party begins. Learn about Houston's Astronomy Day and the annual Texas Star Party in West Texas. Houston astronomers have a strong and on-going community outreach. Take in the daily star show at the Burke Baker Planetarium. Every year more and more activities designed specifically for kids are happening. Amazing worlds beyond our own solar system await you and your child.

Did you know:

- Within the Milky Way 29 planets have been discovered orbiting stars like our own?
- Planet hunters spot their prey by measuring tiny variations of light emitted by distant stars?

- Houston's amateur astronomers have discovered about thirty asteroids from the Fort Bend Observatory?
- A local astronomy club searches for supernova?
- A group of southern searchers looking for extra-solar planets found *three* new planets orbiting stars like our sun in late 2000?

Astronomy, with its math and science, offers children a sense that the world is an ordered place and teaches them to observe things more carefully. Young astronomers learn to classify, to organize, and to conduct experiments. Their curiosity is stimulated, but more important they learn the value of persistence. Best of all is what the Space Center Houston folks say: "You *can* have intelligent fun!"

Space Center Houston

Official Visitors Center of NASA's Johnson Space Center
1601 NASA Road 1, Houston, Texas 77058

Ph: 281-244-2100
Outside Houston: 800-972-0369
Web site: www.spacecenter.org (check the Events Calendar)
Fees: Adults $14.95   Seniors 65+ $13.95
           Children 4-11 $10.95   3 yrs. and under Free
Parking: $3
Winter hours: Weekdays 10 a.m. – 5 p.m. (closed Christmas Day)
           Sat. – Sun. 10 a.m. – 7 p.m.
Summer hours: Open daily 9 a.m. – 7 p.m.
Location: 1601 NASA Road 1, midway between Houston and Galveston off I-45.
Amenities: wheelchairs, RV parking, picnic area, and pet facilities

Call to verify hours of operation. Parking fees, operating hours, show and exhibit schedules are subject to change without notice.

For groups of fifteen or more, call Group Sales at 281-244-2130 or 1-800-972-0369 at least 48 hours in advance to get the discounted rate and make a group reservation.

Recommended Ages: Most programs are geared for pre-kindergarten on up. Many activities for two-year-olds are found in Kids Space Place.

Space Center Houston © Elaine L. Galit, 2000.

Tips:

- If you are planning a visit, call ahead and request the general Space Center Houston brochure. You might also visit their web site so you have a good idea of what to expect. Map out a plan prior to your visit.

- If you *really* want to have the visit be an educational experience for your child, come up with some questions that your child must answer while he or she's visiting but make them the kind that promotes learning. (Visit the web site www.space-center.org.) Two examples are: How much will he or she weigh on Mars? or Who was the first astronaut in space?

- Plan on spending four to six hours at the center. There is a full food court area that serves a variety of foods.

- Best web site is http://spacelink.nasa.gov/.index.html. *Hot Topics* features current events related to NASA, and *Cool Picks* takes you to intriguing and educational NASA materials and sites, but don't stop there. The Library and *Spacelink Express* are great tools.

Space Center Houston, although the Official Visitors Center of NASA's Johnson Space Center (JSC), is not a part of NASA. Space Center is separate and nonprofit, owned and operated by the Manned Space Flight Education Foundation, Inc. They do not receive any federal funding. The JSC's visitor program ended in 1992 when Space Center opened. The center's creators kept in close contact with NASA to ensure the most accurate experience. Each attraction is self-guided so you can spend as much time or as little in each area as desired. Generally, you should plan to spend four to six hours.

Plenty of fun is available for the whole family. You'll see the actual space suits worn by the astronauts, visit a space flight kiosk where you'll attempt to land a shuttle, and try on replicas of space helmets from different time periods. Learn what it's like to live on the space station. You can even get your photograph taken as if you're wearing a space suit. If you get hungry, you can take a break at the Zero G Diner. A Starbucks kiosk is available for coffee lovers. The complex consists of the following:

- *Space Center Plaza*—The plaza is the central hub of activity. Get a close-up look at the flight deck and mid-deck of the Space Shuttle in a full-scale mock-up. A recent exhibit featured the Hubbell Telescope; a future exhibit will be on microbes.

- *Kids Space Place*—The newest addition, this area is totally interactive. A hands-on area geared toward kids and families so all ages can experience the space program firsthand. If you're looking for a great place to take a two-year-old, this is it (allow 30 minutes).

- *Starship Gallery*—Features the world's largest display of moon rocks. You'll relive the triumphs of America's manned space flight program, then trace the progression of the space program in the artifact gallery (allow 30 minutes).

- *Mission Status Center*—Discover up-to-the-minute details on current and future Space Shuttle missions (allow 30 minutes).

- *NASA Tram Tour*—Go behind the scenes of NASA. You'll visit Mission Control and Building 9 where the astronauts train. Trams fill quickly so plan to take a tour early in your visit. During the summer more than one tram runs, but in the fall and spring only one is available. They run every 20-30 minutes (allow 90 minutes if you visit all areas on the tour).

- *Space Center IMAX Theater*—Blast off into a journey through space in Texas's largest 5-story IMAX theater (allow 1 hour).

- *The Feel of Space*—Experience the challenges of living and working in space during this live presentation (allow 45 minutes).

- *Spacetrader Gift Shop*—This is the place if you want an authentically styled flight suit, complete with NASA mission patches. The "Little Astronaut" set includes a full body astronaut suit and a realistic space helmet. Astronaut food, patches, flight jackets, toys, models, videos, everything you could possibly want is available from the gift shop.

- *Special Exhibits, Events*—These are part of the Space Center experience. Exhibits change throughout the year and include a mix of space themes from stellar art to cosmic photographs of space. Call for more information about upcoming exhibits.

All attractions are on a first-come, first-served basis. Trams may be interrupted by inclement weather. The entire party should wait in line. Late seating is not available for most shows, so plan to arrive early.

Space Center Houston. "Roberta Jacobs—space cadet." © Elaine L. Galit, 2000.

Education Programs

The Space Center Houston Education Office's goal is to stimulate children in the area of math and science and to make things fun and exciting for students and for educators. The center provides NASA designed curriculum guides, hands-on activities, fact sheets, and other materials for the classroom. Information is available on field trips, camps, overnights, teacher workshops, and scout programs. Some information follows. To schedule events, call 281-244-2145 or 800-972-0369 x 2145. Information is also on the web site (www.spacecenter.org).

Note: There is a statewide system of Educator Resource Centers. This center is for an eight-state region, but there is also one in Brownsville, Texas, for the same area. Almost all of the fifty states have ERCs.

For the General Public

- *Scout Camp-ins*—These are very structured, which is often a surprise to the participant. Another surprise for the campers is that they are actually learning something while they're having so much fun. The program begins with an overnight in the center. The camper is engaged in a structured evening full of hands-on activities, as well as films and presentations, all designed with the scout badge requirements in mind. These are terrific programs at reasonable rates. Camp-ins available for Boy Scouts, Girl Scouts, and Cub Scouts (Webelos and Bears only). Spaces are limited and fill up fast, so you must register early. *Plan six months ahead for these programs.* Call 281-244-2148 or e-mail acase@spadcenter1.org or visit their web site at www.spacecenter.org for more details.

- *Summer Day Camps*—Parents often comment on their child's excitement after attending one of these camps. The children return home wanting to share what they've learned.

Register early if you want to ensure your child's attendance. Registration normally begins in May, and the camps are often full by June. Each day camp focuses on a different aspect of the space program such as building and launching a model rocket, designing a futuristic space vehicle, constructing and controlling a robot, and making an astronaut helmet. Summer camps are for Astronaut Candidates (5-7 yrs. old), Mission Specialists (8-11 yrs. old), and Shuttle Commanders (12-14 yrs. old). Day camps are for girls and boys ages 5-15. Call early for registration brochures as these fill up *very* fast! Call 281-244-2148 for details and cost.

- *Day Camps*—The week after Christmas and during spring break, Space Center offers day camps for ages 5-11 yrs.

A favorite activity in the day camps program is for 5-to-7-year-olds to make a space suit out of a paper bag. The child colors the suit and uses stickers. He also constructs a small helmet complete with balloon oxygen tanks.

Another favorite is the planet necklace. All the planets are on it, and there are beads that represent the distance between the planets so the child learns about the solar system. They also make a little visor that is the sun and when worn, the sun and solar system orbit around the child's head.

- *Day care program*—available for 2-to-3-year-olds. Contact the group sales office for information on this program.

for Educators

Note: Home school groups and their teachers are welcome at all educator programs and workshops. Call the education department and request brochures on their various offerings.

- *Field Trips/School Groups*—Space Center Houston offers students several types of visits that allow them to experience the "real stuff," including an overnight program for those who must travel a long distance. Field trips can be designed to include IMAX, the Outer Space Academy, and a School

Overnight Program. Or schedule your visit during one of the "special" weeks that allow students to interact with scientists and engineers who work in the space program. (Meet an Astronaut Week, Robots in Space Week, and Training for Space Week are just a few that are offered.) Teachers will receive grade level appropriate classroom activities, descriptions of attractions, exhibits and more. Reserve your group visit at least one month prior to the date you select. Three programs are offered. The center has an information packet that contains maps, lunch information, activities that can be done prior to the visit, and a code of conduct. Call 281-244-2145 or 1-800-972-0369 x 2145 for more information.

Note: Students must be with their chaperone at all times.

- *Professional Development Workshops*—Use space to teach and experience intelligent fun. Educator workshops are held throughout the year for K-12 teachers. Participants receive 6 hours of Continuing Professional Development (CPE) and receive materials to take back to the classroom. These are full day workshops (8:30 a.m. – 3:30 p.m.) that include a visit to the center. Lunch and snacks are provided.

- *International Space Station Educators Conference*—An annual 2-day event that usually occurs the first week of February. Educators come in from all over the country. This is a very popular event. In 2000 there were over 400 attendees and 100 presenters. Presentations are on a variety of topics related to the International Space Station. There is a wide range of speakers and topics and a lot of information and materials available to the attendees. This is a great opportunity for teachers to both learn and enjoy. There is also a banquet and an astronaut band.

- *Annual Open House*—Usually held in September after the facility has closed for the evening. This allows teachers to come in, preview the center, and find out about the various programs. Food, materials, information, and door prizes are all on the agenda. Home school teachers are welcome. (This is an adult event for educators; no children.)

- *Teacher Camp*—This event is for all educators and occurs in April. Teachers stay overnight and sleep in sleeping bags in the Starship Gallery, or they stay up all night and watch sci-fi movies. This is a structured event with many hands-on activities.

For Home Schoolers

Home school groups are considered to be like any other school group. The center recommends that all groups call one month ahead to reserve their visit. The center will then send a confirmation with details, a code of conduct, and information that includes activities that can be done ahead of the visit. During the visit the students must remain with their chaperones at all times.

The home school educator is welcome to attend any of the programs the center offers, as well as the special Home School Days devoted specifically to the home school educator's needs.

- *Home School Days*—Two special days each year are set aside for home school groups only. The center is closed to the public, and home school groups are given the opportunity to have the center to themselves for the entire day. Special educational activities, presentations, curriculum, and pricing are offered on these two days to meet the special needs of home school groups. Call and make a reservation at 281-244-2164.

The first Home School Day resulted in over 5,000 attendees. Information is provided on the center's web site.

NASA Johnson Space Center Tour

Web site: http://jsc.nasa.gov

When you visit Space Center Houston, you may choose to take a tram tour of the Johnson Space Center (JSC). The center occupies more than 16,000 acres and employs more than 14,000 people, including contractors and civil servants.

- JSC is the federal facility, home to the Mission Control Center, where Space Shuttle missions are run from seconds after launch to landing. It is also where astronauts are trained and the Space Shuttle program is managed.

- JSC also directs the International Space Station (ISS) program. The astronauts who will build and live on the ISS train here. JSC is building the X-38, a new spacecraft designed to return the ISS crew to Earth in case of an emergency.

NASA Lyndon B. Johnson Space Center © Vikk Simmons, 2000.

- The Center also studies and cares for more than 800 pounds of lunar rocks and soil collected during the Apollo program.

Johnson Space Center Educator Resource Center

1601 NASA Road 1, Houston, Texas 77058

Hours: Monday – Friday 10 a.m. – 5 p.m.
                   Weekends by appointment
Ph: 281-244-2129 or 1-800-972-0369 x 2129
Fax: 281-483-9638
Web site: www.spacecenter.org

> **Tip:** *Be specific in your request. For example, don't ask for information on the solar system, ask for information on Mars.*

The JSC Educator Resource Center is charged with providing NASA material to educators and not the general public. Their material is classroom oriented. The vast web site materials are the best material for the public. The material on the web is the same as the material offered by the resource center.

> **Note:** All printed material is available on the web site. Because the material is so vast and changes so quickly, this is the only way to keep information updated.

The ERC has many services to assist educators:

- Advisors to help teachers plan units
- Access to a wide variety of NASA curricula for all grade levels and subjects
- Information on additional resources to help support educators in the classroom

- Teacher workshops on a variety of space-related topics
- Astronomy material is basically for 5th–12th grades but every other subject—such as aeronautics, earth science, living in space, physics, mathematics, and of course, the solar system—is K-12.
- Over 100 NASA educational videos are available for educators to view and copy to their own blank tapes.
- All educators, including home school, are urged to use the web site.
- http://core.nasa.gov is the multimedia resource. Through this web site educators can view the catalog and review the topic by media, in other words, by videotape, CD-ROM, and slides.

Houston Museum of Natural Science (HMNS)

One Hermann Circle Drive, Houston, Texas 77030

Ph: 713-639-4600
Web site: www.hmns.org *(terrific web site!)*
Fees: Please call the museum to check pricing as they offer several different package combinations.
Garage Parking: $2 per car
Hours: Monday – Saturday 9 a.m. – 6 p.m.
　　　　Sunday 11 a.m. – 6 p.m.
　　　　Tuesdays after 2:00 p.m. are free
　　　　Tuesdays open until 8 p.m. Mar. 14 – Oct. 24

> *Tip: Check their web site for excellent and easy-to-follow directions from all areas of the city.*

Note: The museum is far larger than most people think. Don't expect to walk through the entire museum in two hours and see everything. Be prepared to spend most of the day if you want to see it all. Once you have your museum ticket you can go back and forth between the museum, IMAX, the Cockrell Butterfly Center, and the planetarium. Take advantage of McDonald's restaurant, bring a picnic lunch and sit in the Rose Garden, or go out to lunch and return.

This is one of the top five visited museums in the nation. Visit the web site for a full calendar of astronomical events, special museum programs, and much more. Questions? Consult their *Ask the Scientist* page.

At the Houston Museum of Natural Science (HMNS), numerous exhibits and programs are offered through the Department of Astronomy, including the Challenger Learning Center, the first of an international network of such facilities that offers participants an opportunity to experience a simulated mission into space. The Burke Baker Planetarium, Challenger Learning Center, and the Isaac Arnold Hall of Science are located at the museum downtown. The Fort Bend County George Observatory and a second Challenger Learning Center, although part of the Houston Museum of Natural Science, are located at Brazos Bend State Park. (The Cockrell Butterfly Center and the museum downtown are discussed in other sections of the book.)

Burke Baker Planetarium

One Hermann Circle Drive, Houston, Texas 77030-1799

Ph: 713-639-4629
Web site: www.hmns.org
Hours: Mon. – Fri.   Noon – 3 p.m.
   Sat. – Sun.   Noon – 5 p.m.
   Closed Christmas Day and Thanksgiving Day
Show times: Times may vary; call and confirm

> *Note:* The Planetarium is located within the Houston Museum of Natural Science, which consists of permanent exhibit halls, Wortham IMAX, Cockrell Butterfly Center, Rock Laser Shows, Collector's Shop, and the Discovery Shop. A visit can easily take up many hours, and a child can make major discoveries.

This is not the same Planetarium it was in the 1970s! The facility has really blossomed. The whole focus is to make astronomy interesting and fun. An out-of-this-world experience awaits visitors. The Planetarium features an array of star-studded programs from Bach to the Beatles. Visitors can experience the world's first digital video sky theater, the most advanced in the world, with full-dome moving images to complement its star field displays. The Digistar star field projector makes it possible to simulate stars, planets, comets, nebulous objects, and other special effects including a 3D flight through space. There are a number of astronomy presentations offered every day and on the weekends. Here's your chance to explore the universe.

- Go to the web site to find out what shows are currently running in the planetarium, IMAX, and if there are any special educational lectures or shows.

- Check out the daily star show, *Stargazer's Guide*, about Houston's night sky. The star show is always age appropriate to the audience that day (weekdays at 3 p.m., weekends and holidays at 5 p.m.—times vary, call to confirm).

- Where is Carmen Sandiego? Find out. The planetarium always offers a Carmen Sandiego show. Carmen may be exploring the solar system or roaming through the universe (every day at noon).

- Special shows such as *Alien Oceans: Journey to Dharmok's Gate* (showing through April 2001), a science fantasy, take you across the galaxy in search of a gateway between universes (weekdays at 1 and 2 p.m., weekends and holidays at 1, 2, 3, and 4 p.m.—call to confirm all show times).

- Birthday parties are available. Call for summer and Saturday camp information.

The Challenger Learning Center

Call 713-639-4629 for more information

Special Mars and Moon missions for children age 9 and up. Children embark on a virtual journey into space. The center is a

Challenger Learning Center. Courtesy of Houston Museum of Natural Science.

good representation of the Mission Control that existed in 1988. The Museum has plans to give the area the blue look of the new Mission Control.

> *Note:* A more detailed explanation of the Challenger Learning Centers is found under the George Observatory at Brazos Bend listing.

Isaac Arnold Hall of Space Science

Here are exhibits that range from a moon rock returned by *Apollo 12* to a Mercury spacecraft that logged a few million miles of outer space travel before settling in the Museum.

Houston Museum of Natural Science [Brazos Bend]

George Observatory at Brazos Bend State Park

The place where kids come with curiosity in their minds and leave with stars in their eyes.

George Observatory Ph: 281-242-3055
HMNS Main Ph: 713-639-4629
Web site: www.hmns.org
Park Entrance Fees: adults $3, children under 12 are free.
Hours: Mon. – Sat.: By reservation only for school and group tours
      Friday: The Observatory can be reserved for groups of 30+
      Call 713-639-4629 to reserve.
Public Viewing: Saturday 3 p.m. – 10 p.m.
      (Public viewing tickets are available at 5 p.m., first come, first served.)

> **Tip:** *Go to the museum's web site (www.hmns.org) for directions. The observatory is located about an hour's drive from Houston in Brazos Bend State Park. The Brazos Bend facilities are part of the Houston Museum of Natural Science (HMNS).*

What is unique about the observatory is that it is an educational facility. Its main purpose is not astronomy but education. The mission is to get people to look up. While it is easy to assume not much is going on at the observatory, that would be a mistake. This is a busy place and a boon for the community. The staff is dedicated, articulate, and full of energy. They want the public to use the observatory and the Challenger Learning Center. In addition, they have forged working relationships with local astronomy organizations and are dedicated to community outreach.

Located at the Museum's satellite facility in Brazos Bend State Park, visitors can observe the heavens through the largest telescope in the nation dedicated to public viewing. The observatory has 3 large telescopes, one of which has a giant 36" mirror.

The Houston Museum of Natural Science built the observatory in 1989. All the staff agrees that the best part about the observatory has to do with all the volunteers. On Saturday night amateur astronomers bring their own telescopes and interact with the public. These volunteers have discovered asteroids; they've searched for supernovas, and they've found peculiar galaxies. Friendly and willing to answer questions, the volunteers help kids learn to love the stars in the night sky as much as they do.

Note: We are convinced that both the George Observatory and the Challenger Learning Center at Brazos Park are hidden jewels waiting to be discovered by the Houston public.

Saturday Night Public Viewing—Calling All Stargazers

Kids enjoy looking at the moon and the planets. Visit the observatory on any Saturday night, when the 10-ton research telescope opens to the public. See the planets, galaxies, and other wonders in our Houston night sky. Most activities are free of charge, except for the 36" research telescope (adults $2, children $1).

The observatory opens to the public at 3 p.m.

Tickets for the big telescope go on sale at 5 p.m., and the park closes at 10 p.m. There are no reservations. There is a talk on the hour, each hour, before you go in to view the sky. Viewing begins when it gets dark, but you must get your pass at 5 p.m.

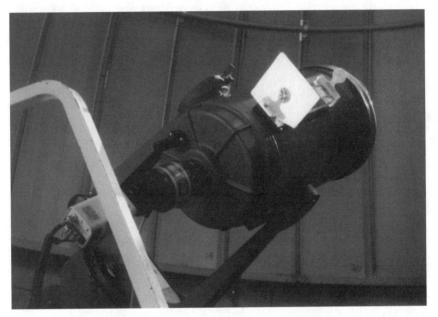

George Observatory telescope. © Elaine L. Galit, 2000.

Tip: Bring a picnic dinner and mosquito repellent. Pick up your pass at 5 p.m., then take advantage of the extra time to check out the park's nature trails and the observatory's interactive exhibits, and talk to the local astronomers.

Did you know:

- You can see the planet Saturn through the big telescope?
- You can see the Milky Way?
- Astronomy Day is in October?

- Want to see the moon? Try the first quarter moon. You don't want a full moon as you need shadows to see the craters.
- Look for Saturn in the fall.

Friday Night Viewing

Groups can reserve the Observatory to view the night sky. Prior to stargazing, the Observatory staff will present a special slide show. By reservation only. Cost: $5 per person, plus 50 cents per person for park entrance fee. *Viewing times are between 7:30 p.m. and 10 p.m.*

Far-out Telescope Viewing, Special Classes, and More!

Groups of kids from all over Texas take advantage of the observatory's classes. Barbara Wilson, the staff astronomer, is accomplished, internationally known, and published. She has the gift of being able to "talk astronomy" to graduate students attending Rice University, kindergartners, and everyone in between. Her enthusiasm for her subject is contagious.

Note: all classes are available to home school groups.

Astronomy Day Classes

The day classes feature hands-on activities covering optics, telescopes, spectroscopes, and other astronomer tools. Solar telescopes allow students to see solar flares and sunspots. There's also a motion demonstration of the 36" research telescope and giant dome (approx. 50 minutes, held Monday-Friday, minimum 20 students, $2.50 per person).

Additional Classes

Our Neighborhood—a tour of the solar system for grades 1-3.

Groups of any age can explore the following classes: *Mars, Deep Space, Hubbell Space Telescope, Visible and Invisible Light, Colorful*

Night Sky. All classes are tailored to match student's grade levels. Cost: $2 per person, plus 50 cents per person for park entrance fee.

Challenger Learning Center at Brazos Park

Come to this "space place" where kids are the crew, facing the real life challenges of a complex space mission. Betty Glass, the observatory's director says, "The missions are spectacular learning tools." Aboard the simulated spacecraft *Observer*, or working on consoles in Mission Control, kids learn teamwork and communication skills while experiencing the thrill of manned space flight.

Give your child an out-of-this-world birthday party. Party includes a space station simulation. Space parties for all ages are available. One woman celebrated her 40th birthday with a simulation and brought a cooler full of Tang. They've conducted Father's Day missions where the sons are signed up and the father flies free. Little kids make great teams with their dads.

Missions teach teamwork, problem solving, and communications, things you aren't always able to cultivate in a classroom setting. Most kids think they have done something really hard and have done it really well. It provides a wonderful sense of accomplishment once the mission is over. Missions last two hours. They are designed to teach science, math, and technology, but the true bonus lies in the life skills that are developed and tested. The mission demonstrates that science is exciting.

- *Full Mission*—Astronauts spend half their time in Mission Control consoles and the other half operating their spacecraft (2 hours, up to 40 students, grades 4-12, cost is $240 per mission plus 50 cents per person for park entrance fee).

- *Mini Mission*—For special or smaller groups, students become astronauts, operating the space craft on their own mission (1 hour, up to 20 students, grades 4-12, cost is $140 per mission plus 50 cents per person for park entrance fee).

- *Junior Mission*—Younger children and their eight adult helpers pilot their spacecraft through deep space (1½ hours, up to 30 students, grades 1-3, cost $175 per mission plus 50 cents per person for park entrance fee).

  Note: Challenger Center experiences begin with classroom training activities and an optional on-site teacher training program. Both the pre-visit materials provided to the teacher, and the mission itself, address TAAS science objectives.

Other Listings

Lone Star Flight Museum (LSFM)

2002 Terminal Drive (Galveston Airport), Galveston, Texas 77554

Ph: 800-582-4673 or 409-740-7722
Fax: 409-740-7612
Web site: www.lsfm.org
Fees: Adults $6   Seniors 65+ $4
          Teens (14-17) $5   Kids (5-13) $4   Under 5 Free
          Memberships and group rates are available
Hours: Daily 10 a.m. – 5 p.m. Closed Christmas
Amenities: Wheelchair accessible, smoke-free, guided tours by appointment, and a museum store

> **Tip:** *The web site (www.lsfm.org) provides links to other aircraft museums and to sites about vintage aircraft.*

Home of the Texas Aviation Hall of Fame, the Lone Star Flight Museum (LSFM) houses the largest collection of historically significant aircraft in the southern United States. LSFM is dedicated to acquiring, restoring to flying condition, and preserving a collection of aircraft, and to the men and women in aviation history.

"Kids Week," fly-ins, and air shows are some of the events they offer. More than 40 aircraft are displayed, most of which have been restored to flying condition. In addition to vintage aircraft, kids programs, lectures, and exhibits are offered. Group tours are welcome. Available after hours for private receptions.

Note: The Lone Star Museum has a partnership with the Houston Museum of Natural Science.

Moody Gardens Discovery Pyramid

Living in the Stars: Explore the Future in Outer Space
One Hope Boulevard, Galveston, Texas 77554

Ph: 800-582-4673
Fax: 409-744-1631
Web site: www.moodygardens.com
Fees: Call for current pricing as they have several packages available. You may also purchase a special Day Pass.
Summer Hours: Open daily from 10 a.m. – 9 p.m.
Except December 25th
Winter Hours: Sun. –Thurs.   10 a.m. – 6 p.m.
Fri. & Sat.   10 a.m. – 8 p.m.
Last admission one hour before closing
Amenities: lockers, strollers, and wheelchairs, first aid and diaper changing facilities. Gift shop and dining services provided. Membership passes provide unlimited free admission and members-only events for one year. Available at the Visitor Information Center.
Attraction tickets: Available at all ticket booths. Ticket booths open at 9:30 a.m.

The Moody Gardens complex consists of three pyramids: a 10-story Rainforest Pyramid, an Aquarium Pyramid, and the Discovery Pyramid dedicated to space exploration. Travel across space and time to discover how we will live and work among the stars. You'll find more than 30 interactive exhibits, designed in cooperation with NASA's Johnson Space Center, and a fun-filled science theater.

Moody Gardens "Mission control" Discovery Pyramid. © Elaine L. Galit, 2000.

Step aboard the International Space Station and explore the Habitation Module to understand what happens to people during long periods of time in space. See what the X-38 Space Station Escape Pod looks like. Try docking the Space Shuttle with Space Station Mir at the Docking Trainer. This is the same program practiced by real astronauts. Finally, check out Shuttle Theater where upcoming Space Shuttle missions are broadcast via satellite link to NASA-TV.

IMAX Ridefilm Theater—Strap on your seatbelt for a moving and shaking adventure in film viewing. Hold on as the 180-degree wraparound screen puts you right in the action.

Note: Admission to the IMAX 3D Theater is $7. Call for show times.

Education Programs for Groups

Call 800-582-4673 or 409-744-4673 Ext. 4332
for information and reservations

Moody Gardens offers a number of educational programs including outreach, educator, and field trip, as well as special programs designed specifically for scouts, overnight adventures, kids camps, birthdays, and star parties.

Reservations are required for all education programs at least two weeks in advance and are taken on a first-come, first-served basis. Adult chaperones are required to accompany groups at all times. Groups are welcome to bring their lunches or make reservations for the lunch packages available at Moody Gardens. Call for information on programs designed for educators.

Star Parties

See the Stars! Get a firsthand look at the rings of Saturn or the moons of Jupiter. Moody Gardens and the Johnson Space Center Astronomical Society will help you explore the heavens. Telescopes are provided and experienced astronauts are on hand to answer questions. Call for dates. Parties last from dusk until 11 p.m. and are free.

 Toolbox Tips

Using Space Center and NASA Web Sites

Because the informational material is so vast and constantly changing, the web site is the best way to acquire the data. You can download mountains of material from the sites. For educators and children, they recommend the Space Link, http://spacelink.com.

Star Parties

Houston has several strong and active astronomy groups. Star parties are frequent in Houston and throughout Texas. The groups are:

Fort Bend Astronomy Club
   Web site: http://rampages.onramp.net/~binder
   E-mail: binder@onramp.net
   Fort Bend Astronomy Club
   P.O. Box 942, Stafford, Texas, 77497-0942

Houston Astronomical Society
   Web site: http://spacsun.rice.edu/~has
   E-mail: goldberg@sccsi.com (Steve Goldberg)
   Houston Astronomical Society
   Attn: Society Information
   P.O. Box 20332, Houston, Texas 77225-0332
   Ph: 281-568-9340 (recording)

Johnson Space Center Astronomical Society
   Web site: http://www.ghg.net/cbr/jscas/
   E-mail: jscas@ghg.net

North Houston Astronomy Club
   Web site: http://www.astronomyclub.org/
   (This is a new club, only in existence for about a year.)
   E-mail: astrobil@flash.net or bill.leach@nhmccd.edu
   Snail mail: Bill Leach
   Kingwood College
   20000 Kingwood Dr.
   Kingwood, Texas 77339-3801
   Ph: Bill Leach 281-312-1650 (W) 713-863-8459 (H)

Astronomical Society of Southeast Texas
   (No web site)
   P.O. Box 7943, Beaumont, Texas 77706

Take a Journey to Any Place in the Universe

Combine imagination with a few facts, and any child can plan a journey to any place in the universe. Use evening story time to read books on Mars, Jupiter, Saturn, and their moons. Ask your child what he or she would need in order to live on their favorite planet. A Martian might breath dust, a Venusian would live in a shallow bowl, due to the dense surface that appears to curve upwards, and a Plutonian would need a great furnace and a lot of electric light.

Keep a Space Journal

Have your child keep a journal. Each night have him or her write about the trip: where they are going, what they are taking with them, and how they are feeling about the trip. If you're going to Mars you might want a space suit, oxygen, food, and a radio. Your child can also draw pictures of the planet and what they might see, what type of alien life forms they might encounter.

Begin a Logbook

Encourage your child to begin a logbook right away. Like all good scientists, the child will want to keep a record of activities done, places visited, and questions that have been answered. It's a record of their personal space journey.

Watch NASA-TV

You may not know it, but if you have cable or a satellite dish you can watch NASA-TV. You'll see live missions and educational programs. Interactive distance learning programs are available through the Internet at http://nasa.gov.ntv.

Star Maps and Telescopes

One of the first things most budding astronomers acquire is a star map. Due to Houston's high humidity, it is a good idea to purchase a plastic map and not a paper one. Another favorite item is a telescope. Start kids off with a simple telescope. Most experts agree that the telescopes should be purchased from a recognized astronomy outlet or from a company such as Land, Sea and Sky where the quality of the instrument is much higher and the staff more knowledgeable than a mall store or a catalogue.

- For some hands-on experience with a refracting telescope, try the Refracting Telescope Kit offered by Project STAR, a division of Learning Technologies, Inc. It's a simple refractor with plastic lenses mounted in a cardboard tube. When assembled, it's a 16x refractor capable of revealing lunar craters and Jupiter's moons. No glue is needed and the scope can be assembled and disassembled over and over—a plus for classroom teachers.

For more information on the Project STAR telescopes, which can be bought in bulk, contact Learning Technologies, Inc., 40 Cameron Avenue, Somerville, MA 02144 *Ph:* 800-537-8703; or you can check out their web site at www.starlab.com/.

On the Web

Go to www.astromy.com and click on "Astro for Kids." Learn about the planets in our solar system and click on the images of the planets to discover more about their special characteristics.

Resources

Books, Brochures, Magazines, and Information

Astronomy Magazine
www.astronomy.com

Sky & Telescope Magazine
www.skyandtelescope.com

How to Access Information on NASA's Education Program, Materials and Services NASA Office of Human Resources & Education. EP-1999-06-345-HQ

Information Services Center (ISC) The ISC handles requests for crew pictures and NASA information. Students and the public can also send requests for information to: ISC, Johnson Space Center, AP2, 2101 NASA Road 1, Houston, Texas 77058-3696, or call 281-483-8693, or *e-mail:* infoserc@jsc.nasa.gov.

JSC Student Programs Internet site listing academic and career opportunities available to high school and college students at Johnson Space Center. http://students.jsc.nasa.gov/ and http://coop.jsc.nasa.gov/.

Suggested Books for Preschool-Early Grades

- *Sun, Moon & Stars* by Mary Hoffman. Interesting book combining space with different mythologies.
- *See the Stars: Your First Guide to the Night Sky* by Ken Croswell. Very good! Picks one prominent constellation for each month. Good introduction to deep sky objects (galaxies, nebula, double stars, etc.).
- *Scholastic's Encyclopedia of Space* by Jacqueline and Simon Mitton

- *The Everything Kids' Space Book: All About Rockets, Moon Landings, Mars & More Plus Space Activities Your Can Do at Home!* by Kathiann Kowalski (good for grades 1-5)
- *Zoo in the Sky: A Book of Animal Constellations* by Jacqueline Mitton

Middle Grades

- *How the Universe Works* by Heather Couper. Good book from basic solar system to black holes and quantum physics.
- *DK Space Encyclopedia* by Heather Couper. Good; from basic solar system information to black holes and quantum physics.
- *Astronomy Today: Planets, Stars, Space Exploration* by Harry McNaught & Dinah Moche. Good overview of all things astronomical from planets to galaxies.

For Teens and Adults

- SETI@home-online. System that searches for signs of extraterrestrial intelligence.
- *Sky at Night: Your Guide to the Heavens* by Robin Kerrod. Good beginner's kit! Durable plastic star map, red flashlight (so you won't ruin your night vision), and two beginner books.
- *Failure is Not an Option* by Gene Kranz
- *40 Nights to Learning the Sky* by Fred Schaaf. Similar to Croswell's *See the Stars for Adults*. One constellation, planet, or deep sky object per night. Overviews of how the Earth moves through the universe, etc.
- *Star-Hopping: Your Visa to Viewing the Universe* by Robert Garfinkle. Good introduction to finding deep sky objects & navigating. Must have binoculars or telescope.
- *Star Ware: The Amateur Astronomer's Ultimate Guide to Choosing & Buying Telescopes & Accessories* by Phillip S. Harrington. Though geared for the serious amateur, everyone should take a

look at this guide before they buy. Avoid the common pitfalls of discount/department store shopping. Figure out what you need (and see all the stuff you probably don't).

General Web Sites

www.Astronomy.com
New to astronomy? Go to this web site. Up-to-date news, photographs, featured stories, even samples of the current issue of *Astronomy Magazine* are available. Click on "For Beginners," "Astrokids," and the page for parents and educators.

Starchild
http://starchild.gsfc.nasa.gov
Site with information on the solar system and space travel for children. Games and activities are included.

NASA's Discovery Program
http://discovery.nasa.gov
Learn about the exciting missions and their many "first-ever" events. Each mission web site has great educational activities for students of all ages. (Mars Pathfinder, Lunar Prospector, NEAR, Stardust, Genesis, CONTOUR, MESSENGER, and Deep Impact.)

Mars Millennium Project
http://www.mars2030.net/
A national arts, sciences, and technology education initiative

NASA for Kids
www.nasa.gov/kids.html
Cool NASA sites for students

LSDA's Just for Kids
http://lsda.jsc.nasa.gov
Games and activities about space flight

NASA Student Involvement Program
www.nsip.net
National program of investigations and design challenges

Space Science News
http://science.nasa.gov
Latest in Space Science News—designed for older students

NASA Homepage
www.nasa.gov

Space Telescope Science Institute
www.stsci.edu/EPA/Pictures.html
The STSI has information on and pictures from the Hubble
Space Telescope. Educational materials and activities are available at *Amazing Space.*

Earth from Space
http://earth.jsc.nasa.gov

JSC Homepage
www.jsc.nasa.gov/

JSC Digital Image Collection
www.nasa.gov/gallery/index.html

International Space Station and Space Shuttle
http://spaceflight.nasa.gov

Mission Control
www.jsc.nasa.gov/pao.factsheets/nasapubs/mccfact.html

NASA Image eXchange
http://nix.nasa.gov/nix.cgi
Search engine for accessing NASA online image and photo
collections

Lunar Prospector
http://lunar.arc.nasa.gov/
Contains information on NASA's latest mission to the moon

Planetary Probes
www.jpl.nasa.gov/

Satellites/Earth Science
www.gsfc.nasa.gov/

NASA History
www.hq.nasa.gov/office/pao/History/history.html

Early U.S. Manned Flight
http://riceinfo.rice.edu/Fondren/Woodson/jsc-archive.html

Life Sciences Data Archive
http://lsda.jsc.nasa.gov/
Information, photos, videos about space flight experiments

Lunar and Planetary Institute
http://cass.jsc.nasa.gov/
Share in the excitement of space exploration

Planetary Data Systems
http://pds.jpl.nasa.gob/edu.html
Links to educational resources related to planets and astronomy

National Space Science Data Center
http://nssdc.gsfc.nasa.gov/
Access information about astrophysics, space physics, and more

Space Telescope Science Institute
http://marvel.stsci.edu/
Contains the latest news and information about Hubble Space Telescope activities

Advanced Life Support Program
http://pet.jsc.nasa.gov/
Information available on research projects, systems to produce food, water, or air

For Educators — Web Sites

Astronomical Society of the Pacific
Their *Project ASTRO* program pairs 4th - 9th grade teachers
with local amateur and professional astronomers.

NASA On-Line Educational Resources
http://education.nasa.gov
NASA's home page serves as a cyber-gateway to information
regarding educational programs and services offered by NASA
for the American educational community.

NASA Spacelink
http://spacelink.nasa.gov
NASA Spacelink, a "virtual library," is one of NASA's electronic resources specifically developed for the educational
community. Hundreds of NASA Web links are arranged in a
manner familiar to educators. A complete listing of NASA
educational products can be found at http://spacelink.nasa
.gov/products.

NASA's Learning Technologies Project
http://education.nasa.gov/ltp
LTP is an agency asset that includes a suite of standards-based
Internet projects that teachers and students can use to explore
and become involved in NASA missions.

NASA Television (NTV)
http://spacelink.nasa.gov/education.file
Go to http://www.nasa.gov/ntv/ntvweb.html to learn about
NASA-TV on the web. NTV features Space Shuttle mission
coverage, live special events, interactive educational live
shows, electronic field trips, aviation and space news, and historical NASA footage.

Teaching Earth Science
www.earth.nasa.gov/education/
Earth science education programs/resources

NASA CORE
  http://core.nasa.gov/
  NASA multimedia educational materials

NASA's Quest Project
  http://quest.arc.nasa.gov
  Bringing the Internet into the classroom

Windows to the Universe
  www.windows.umich.edu/
  Earth and space sciences educator resources

Live from Earth and Mars
  www.k12atmos.washington.edu/k12
  K-12 teaching tools/curricular materials

ALLSTAR Network
  www.allstar.fiu.edu/
  Aeronautics science/research links

The Space Educators Handbook
  http://tommy.jsc.nasa.gov/~woodfill/SPACEED/SEHHTML/
  Links to innovative and unique space education resources

Athena: Earth and Space Science for K-12
  http://athena.webnet.edu
  Instructional materials for classroom use on weather, space, and more

Project Space
  http://learn.jpl/nasa.gov/ProjectSPACE
  Curriculum-support models

The CERES S'COOL Project
  http://asd-www.larc.nasa.gov/SCOOL/
  The Clouds and the Earth's Radiant Energy System—a hands-on project that supports NASA research on the Earth's climate

2

Bugs, Bats, and Butterflies!

T he world is an amazing place, and children are filled with curiosity. Why does a frog leap? How does a spider spin its web? Wondering and thinking is the beginning of all scientific discoveries. By nurturing your child's curiosity, you can propel him into a lifelong voyage of exploration and enjoyment. Encourage your child to turn over a log and lift a rock to see what's underneath. These hands-on adventures excite children.

Science breakthroughs happen because someone won't stop asking why. Children want to know the world. They seek to learn all about plants and animals, rocks and stars, electricity and gravity. Children are junior scientists. They watch, they collect, they compare and classify things. They even predict and come up with their own reasons why. Watch any child and you'll soon see them performing their own simple experiments.

Give a child an inexpensive magnifying glass, a small notebook, a pencil, and a ruler, and you've given them the first tools of scientific discovery. As a boy, Thomas Edison, celebrated inventor and scientist, set up a lab in the basement and learned science at home. Edison was home schooled nearly 150 years ago. The single best thing his mother did was to encourage his questions.

Luckily, Houston is a city with vast resources. Although the city has a reputation for only having a landscape of freeways and overpasses and nothing more, a second look will find a city that knows the value of green. Nestled quietly in a residential area, tucked off a main traffic artery, the Edith L. Moore Nature Sanctuary is waiting to be discovered. Standing seventy feet tall, the Cockrell Butterfly Center recreates a Central American rainforest and maintains a perfect environment for hundreds of species of butterflies.

In the following pages we've tried to give you an idea of the vast and wonderful opportunities that are found throughout the Houston area in the world of life sciences. Visits to any of these places will stimulate a child and provide new discoveries and insights. Did you know:

- In some cultures live beetles become living pendants? People glue stones onto the beetle's back, attach a chain, and pin them onto shirts. The beetle, pinned to the wearer's shoulder, walks around like a "beetle-on-a-leash." See all kinds of beetles at the Insect Zoo when you visit the Cockrell Butterfly Center.

- The armadillo used to be Texas-sized? Native to Houston, these 6 feet long, 3 feet tall ancient armadillos lived tens of thousands of years ago. In 1955 a Houston schoolteacher and two children discovered the bones of one of these creatures. The small armadillos that now populate Texas are originally from South America. See the Texas-sized armadillo bones at the Houston Museum of Natural Science.

- A penguin might be an artist? Check out the penguin art at the Moody Gardens Aquarium and see the penguins in their habitat.

- Texas has a beetle that is 2-3 inches in length? It's called *Dynastes tityus*, the Hercules beetle, and is related to the scarab beetles. The males have ferocious-looking horns, and these beetles are often found flying around street lights or porch lights in the spring and summer. You can see some of them on display at the Insect Zoo of the Cockrell Butterfly Center.

Edith L. Moore Nature Sanctuary

Audubon Docent Guild Services
the Houston Audubon Society
440 Wilchester Blvd., Houston, Texas 77079

Ph: 713-464-4900
Web site: www.houstonaudubon.org/history.html or
www.io.com/~pdhulce/audubon/txtrips.html

The Sanctuary is open and free to the public. Gates open daily at 9 a.m. and close at sunset.

The Audubon Docent Guild Services was founded to provide tours of the 18-acre sanctuary. Although other programs and services are provided, the tours are the main focus. Nominal fees are charged for the various programs such as the *Discover Nature Field Trips, Titmouse Club,* school and home school groups, cabin rentals, birthday parties, and other outreach programs.

The offices, cabin, and library are open to the public weekdays.

Note: Did you know some Houston children have never seen a squirrel? Squirrels need trees. Kids who live on the rice plains, on the Katy prairie, or in Sugar Land often don't have trees.

Tucked away in a residential area north of the Beltway sits a nature paradise waiting to be discovered by children. The Edith L. Moore Nature Sanctuary offers a getaway from the noise and traffic of daily life. With over a mile of trails, visitors find a quiet place to come and enjoy nature. In the spring, migrations of songbirds fill the sanctuary. Hummingbirds abound. Milkweed feeds monarch butterflies, and children use binoculars to identify birds and listen to their songs. Crayfish, tadpoles, frogs, and turtles, even fallen leaves, reveal their secrets under a child's small plastic magnifying glass. Kids walk the bumpy trail and go up and down little rolling hills. Near the cabin, swamp rabbits hang out. Red ear slider turtles bask on logs that stick out of the ponds. Armadillos dig holes in the trails for kids to find. Skinks and geckos scamper.

The operative word is *sanctuary*. This is not a park. "The animals live here. This is their home," says Betty Henderson. "You're not allowed to pick up anything or take anything out of the sanctuary." There are three ponds. If you go through the sanctuary on a guided tour, the docent will supply dip nets and aquariums and show the children turtles, frogs, and tadpoles. Everything is returned to its natural habitat immediately after the demonstration. Everyone connected with the sanctuary demonstrates a deep respect for nature.

Edith L. Moore had lived on the property since 1931 in the log cabin built by herself and her husband. The historic cabin, a genuine log cabin, is now used for the sanctuary's educational programs. Mrs. Moore wished to keep her cabin and surrounding property as a nature sanctuary for school children. She strongly believed in giving city kids a chance to experience the wonders of nature. Each year visitors enjoy the sights and sounds of Rummel Creek, birding on the trails, and looking for turtles and frogs in the pond.

Edith Moore Sanctuary "Log Cabin." © Elaine L. Galit, 2000.

The sanctuary does not receive any public funding. The Houston Audubon Society acquired 18 acres of land along Rummel Creek in 1975.

Tips:

- Great birthday parties are available. October, November, April, and May are the most popular months; call early to schedule a party.

- Tours with docents are available for a minimum of 3-4 people and last about one hour.

- The best times to see swamp bunnies and squirrels are early in the morning and at dusk.

- Take a night walk on the wild side: go on an *Owl Prowl*. The sanctuary offers four walks a year (December, January, February, and March).

Do's and Don'ts

- *Do* wear comfortable, weather appropriate clothing, including closed toe shoes.

- *Don't* bring water bottles. Do use the water fountain. If you have to carry a water bottle, you can't do fun things along the trails.

- *Don't* go off the trails. You can damage the plants.

- *Do* bring a sack lunch. You can sit on the benches. No picnic tables are available.

- *Don't* bring turtles, rabbits, goldfish, or other pets to the sanctuary to release them.

- *Do* remember the creek sides are steep and children could easily slip on dry leaves and have a bad fall.

- *Do* bring bread or saltine crackers but *only* to feed the turtles.

Suggested Activities:

- Make bark or leaf rubbings.

- Bring a nature journal or sketchpad and sit on the decking or at the pond and write and/or draw.

- Turn over logs after a recent rain. Don't catch the spiders, but don't worry as there will be plenty of other things scurrying away.

- Look for different patterns in nature: bark, leafings, spider webs, bugs, even feathers on the trail.

- Keep a sharp eye for wildlife. Play "I spy."

- Have your child bring an inexpensive camera. Photography helps children with their memories.

Cabin Rentals

This genuine log cabin is available for memorials, weddings, and meetings, business or other types. The fee depends on the activity, length of time in the cabin, the number of people, and the type of party. Call for fees.

Programs and Tours

Docent Tours—Anyone can make arrangements for a docent-led tour. Call ahead—a month is suggested—as the volunteer docents must be scheduled. Suitable for all ages, 4-adult. $1.50 donation per person, payable in advance. The group size limit is 60 (which would be divided into smaller groups of 15). They *will* do small groups of 3-4. Tours last an hour with 40 minutes in the woods and 15-20 minutes at the ponds to see if they can catch anything. The docent will provide the dip nets and the aquariums. Kids might want to bring an inexpensive camera, magnifying glass, and binoculars.

> **Note:** A titmouse is a small gray bird with a white breast and a perky gray crest on its head, hence its full name "tufted titmouse." Titmice hang out with chickadees year round in most of Houston's wooded parks and backyards.

Titmouse Club—This club is designed for preschoolers aged 2½-5 years old and is held mid-September through mid-May. Donation is $3 per child. (They *cannot* make change for large bills. They do sell cards for 5 prepaid sessions for $15, but a prepaid card *does not* guarantee a place.) An adult must stay with each child or family. The club meets on Tuesday and Wednesday mornings during the school year, 10 a.m. – 11 a.m. except Thanksgiving week and the three weeks during the Christmas/New Year season. These are science-based classes. Each session features a different nature theme, concentrating on Houston area's animals and habitats. Each session has nature stories, an activity, and a walk in the woods, all led by a volunteer docent. Both Tuesday and Wednesday sessions each week will present the same nature topic. Kids are not water soluble, therefore sessions are held rain or shine. Topics range from hummingbirds, bats, and spiders, to animal tracks, bird feeders, and mushrooms.

Note: Each session is limited to 20 children. No reservations. First come, first served.

Birthday Parties—Children make a nature craft (take-home party favor), take a walk in the woods, go pond dipping, and play nature games. These are great parties. They are offered late August through May, depending on cabin and docent availability. The party is led by two experienced volunteer docents and lasts two hours. There is a 16-child maximum (including the birthday child). Docents lead a dip-and-net down by the pond. Parents furnish all food, paper goods, and utensils. Suitable for children 4-10. Crafts range from making a bat mask to creating a bird's nest. You choose from ten crafts offered. *Fee:* $100 for Monday - Friday parties; $125 for Saturday and Sunday.

Nature Explorers Day Camp—Held during four summer weeks from 9 a.m. – 12 noon, Monday – Friday. Each day features a different nature theme and activities. (Each week is the same.) For children 5-10. Fee was $85/week in 2000. Call early for fee and reservation.

Camp Tadpole—Held for two summer weeks, 9 a.m. – 11 a.m., Monday – Friday. The child can experience a different nature theme and activities each day. (Each week is the same.) For children 4-5 years old. Fee was $60/week in 2000. Call early for fee and reservation.

Pond Camp—This is a great one and not to be missed. One summer week only, 9 a.m. – 12 noon, Monday – Friday. Concentration on pond studies with related activities. For children 9-11, limited enrollment. Fee was $85/week in 2000. Call early for fee and reservation.

Owl Prowls—Enjoy a nighttime owl program in the log cabin beginning with a slide show and talk, followed by a woods prowl to call up screech owls. Each family or group is limited to four reservations. Fee is $5 per person. Minimum age is 6. Given only once a month (December – March). Maximum number of participants is 26.

Outreach Programs—The main focus is on birds. Programs include live birds, slide shows, and stuffed birds. Five different "have-birds-will-travel" programs are available. No auditorium type classes are held due to the live

Edith Moore Sanctuary "Whoo?" says the stuffed owl perched in the log house.
© Elaine L. Galit, 2000.

birds and style of presentation. Smaller groups are preferred because the program consists of hands-on experience, but they are flexible with schools. For adults or children. Fee is $50 for a one-hour presentation. K and 1st grade programs are tailored to their level and cost $25. There is also a daily rate of $200 for up to five programs.

Docent Training—Offered in the spring and fall. For two Saturdays docents-to-be learn about the sanctuary's history, wildlife, and habitat. They are always looking for volunteers.

Programs for Educators
(schools and home schools)

Elementary school classroom and library visits with nature programs are arranged upon request, depending on docent and program availability. Fee is $50 per program.

Discover Nature Field Trips—These classes are provided by the Houston Audubon Society and presented at the sanctuary. They are designed for elementary school students. They are also appropriate for preschool and middle school groups. The units comply with Texas Essential Knowledge and Skills for science, mathematics, language arts, and social studies. (TEKS, mandated by the Texas Education Agency, are the requirements for what must be taught in each subject for every grade level.) This is an interdisciplinary field study program. Classes investigate nature outdoors using scientific methodology and use hands-on activities and games to expand their experience and knowledge. A variety of programs are offered that range from bird watching to habitats, migration to silent hunters. Teachers are also given follow-up packages that provide additional activities and resources on the subjects. Call The Houston Audubon Society at 713-932-1639 ext. 15 for more information and reservations.

- Programs scheduled on a first-come, first-served basis. Scheduled during school hours, Monday – Friday. Most last 1½ hours.

- Cost is $3 per student with a $10 deposit paid at time of registration.

- Maximum number of students is 40. One adult chaperone is required for every 5 preschool to kindergarten students or for every 10 first grade students and older.

School and Home School Groups—They prefer groups of 15-60, although if someone calls with 10 children in the group, they will try to accommodate them. The fee is $3 per child. The programs are flexible. If a group is studying specific issues like conservation or birding, the program can be tailored to fit the group's needs.

Scout Groups—Working on a birding patch? A program can be designed where different stations can teach how to use binoculars, bird identification, feathers, and bird calls. Talks about migration and live birds can be shown. Tell them your needs and they will try to tailor the program to match.

Houston Museum of Natural Science

One Hermann Circle Drive, Houston, Texas 77030

Ph: 713-639-4629

Web site: www.hmns.org *(good web site!)*

Fees: There are a number of fees for various packages that may include other museum attractions. Please contact the Cockrell Center for more information.

Garage Parking: $2 per car

Hours: Mon. – Sat. Opens at 9 a.m.
　　　　Sunday　　　Opens at 11 a.m.

Note: Closing times vary. Call 713-639-4629 for show times and information.

Accessibility Programs: For information about captioning, ASL interpreters, audio descriptions, and other options call 713-639-4629 or 713-639-4687 (TTY) or visit the Museum Services desk. All areas in the museum are wheelchair accessible.

> *Tip: The web site is excellent and provides easy-to-follow directions from all areas of the city.*

Note: The museum is a large place. Don't expect to see everything in two hours. Be prepared to spend most of the day if you want to see all the exhibits. After you buy your museum ticket, you can go back and forth between the museum, IMAX, the Cockrell Butterfly Center, or the planetarium. Take advantage of the McDonalds restaurant or bring a picnic lunch. You can sit in the Rose Garden or go out to lunch and return.

Home to thousands of exotic live butterflies, this three-story glass structure replicates the rainforests in Central America and is designed to be an interactive experience. Be prepared to have butterflies flutter by and occasionally land on you. But first you'll discover what can only be described as a "bug zoo."

49

Children find the Insect Zoo one of their favorite places in the museum. According to J.B. Howell, entomologist, "Kids aren't usually afraid of insects. It's something that you grow into, so they usually enjoy the zoo." He says the fear of insects tends to result from observed behavior. The child watches the parent go "eek!" and then picks up on the parent's behavior. Once in a while, you'll see a child who has an innate fear of insects. A toddler may be completely terrified of a butterfly, but that response is rare.

You'll find docents eager to tell you tales about bugs and butterflies, ready to show you where that hissing roach lives or that beautiful, rare butterfly sits. Want to know what gives a butterfly its color? They're happy to talk about the powdery scale that provides pigment and reflected color, and they're eager to share their knowledge with you and with the children.

Before You Visit: Check out a general insect book from the library. Your child will learn a little bit about the life history of butterflies (egg, caterpillar, and butterfly chrysalis) and will enjoy the experience all the more.

The Insect Zoo and the Brown Hall of Entomology

Surprise: Bugs are beautiful!
See the shiny, beautiful beetles on display.

Located in the lower level of the Cockrell Butterfly Center, the "bug zoo" allows kids to get up close with arthropods. Insects have six legs. More than 30 species, including giant beetles, exotic walking sticks, and those wonderful hissing roaches from Madagascar (sometimes described as "little armadillos") make up this fascinating and diverse collection. For cockroach fans, you'll find species from all over the world. The butterflies may be beautiful, but wait until you see the delicate beauty of giant silk moths and the brilliant sheen of the scarab beetles.

> *Tip: There is a stunning showcase of camouflage insects as part of the Insect Zoo. There are excellent books for children on how insects camouflage and mimic. This is a great exhibit that allows children to really see nature in action.*

Cockrell Butterfly Center

Surprise: Do you know a caterpillar is an immature butterfly? Many children are surprised to learn that those caterpillars they've been squishing are baby butterflies. Not only that, they're insects.

Since it opened in 1994, one of the main goals of the Cockrell Butterfly Center has been to promote butterfly watching, butterfly gardening, and other aspects of butterfly conservation. The center maintains a "perfect butterfly environment." Maintained at 80 degrees and 80 percent humidity, the center is also free of all predators. The butterfly population is kept between 1,500 and 2,000. At any one time you may see about fifty different species, although they bring in upwards of 200 species. Because of their short life spans—average two weeks—there is a constant influx of various species. Young butterflies are released twice a day, morning and evening, and take an hour or two to expand and dry their wings, so they have to sit still for a bit. Supplies of fruit are scattered throughout the center, as well as sugar-water and nectar supplying plants.

Finally, don't be surprised if you see the following sign: *Please watch for stowaways when you're leaving the butterfly habitat.* Make sure when you leave the butterfly area you aren't inadvertently carrying butterflies out.

> *Tip: Best time to see the butterflies is 10 a.m. – 2 p.m. on a non-cloudy day; if cloudy the butterflies are less active.*

Surprise: A butterfly has a chrysalis, which is its exoskeleton. A moth forms a cocoon.

Do's and Don'ts

- *Do* be careful where you walk; don't squash the butterflies.
- *Do* wear colorful clothing; Hawaiian shirts are great.
- *Don't* chase the butterflies if you want them to land on you. Stand still.
- *Do* remember that the more you handle insects, the shorter their life span.
- *Don't* touch the butterflies because the oils in your hands aren't good for them.
- *Do* take a look at the brochures and ask for the one-page "Cockrell Butterfly Center Guide to Butterfly Gardening in the Southern USA," all provided free of charge.

Is there a difference between a butterfly and a moth? There are exceptions to every rule, but generally a butterfly likes to have its wings folded straight above it, while a moth will put its wings in a

Cockrell Butterfly Center at Houston Museum of Natural Science.
One of the inhabitants takes in the sun while resting on a leaf. © Elaine L. Galit, 2000.

Cockrell Butterfly Center at Houston Museum of Natural Science. Take another look and find the caterpillars. © Elaine L. Galit, 2000.

kind of tent over the back of its body, or it likes to sit with its wings open. Moth's bodies are usually heavier, their antennas fuzzy. It's a myth to say that moths are drab. There is a very good display of butterflies and moths in the exhibit hall that is well worth the time spent.

Education Programs

If you enjoy the Cockrell Center, the Insect Zoo, and all the other wonderful facilities such as the planetarium and the exhibits, consider becoming a museum member. Many programs are offered for children throughout the year, including their annual *Hug-a-Bug* event. Because butterflies are insects, the center must use biological control and natural enemies to control pests and plants. Everyone who comes into the center receives a vial of ladybugs, then goes into the butterfly habitat and releases the ladybugs. The event includes a talk about natural predators.

Moody Gardens – Galveston Island

Visitors Center

One Hope Boulevard, Galveston, Texas 77554

Ph: 800-582-4673
Fax: 409-744-1631
Web site: www.moodygardens.com
Fees: Call for current pricing as they have several packages available. You may also purchase a special Day Pass.
Summer Hours: Open daily from 10 a.m. – 9 p.m.
Except December 25th
Winter Hours: Sun. – Thurs. 10 a.m. – 6 p.m.
Fri. – Sat. 10 a.m. – 8 p.m.
Last admission one hour before closing
Attraction tickets: Available at all ticket booths. Ticket booths open at 9:30 a.m.

> *Note:* One of the Education Department's goals is that every person who comes to Moody Gardens walks away with something new, fun, and interesting, a take-a-way.

First stop on any visit to Moody Gardens is the Visitors Center. They can give you more information about Moody Gardens, the education programs, memberships, and the volunteer programs. Their staff is trained and ready to help. The Visitors Center includes the IMAX® 3D Theater, Guest Services Area, Nature's Wonder Gift Shop, Garden Lobby, Preview Theater, Garden Restaurant, the Dancing Waters Fountain, and the Ticket Booth.

> *Tip:* Ask for the Moody Gardens Map & Guide brochure.

Moody Gardens is a nonprofit organization encompassing 242 acres on Galveston Island. Thirty-six percent of the voters in the *City Search—the Best of Houston* poll selected Moody Gardens as the

Sign outside Visitors Center at Moody Gardens.
© Vikk Simmons, 2000.

most enjoyable tourist attraction. This fun-filled, educational destination is comprised of three main pyramids. In this section, we will discuss two of the pyramids—the Rainforest and the Aquarium. Please go to the Space section for detailed information about the Discovery Pyramid.

There's a whole world to discover at Moody Gardens. Explore the Aquarium without getting wet. Experience the rainforests of Africa, Asia, and the Americas in the 10-story glass Rainforest Pyramid. Strap in and hold on as your seat moves with the action in the IMAX® Ridefilm Theater. Reach out and touch as 3-D images leap from the 6-story screen in the IMAX® Theater. Take advantage of the lunch gardens, the Garden Restaurant, and the Aquarium food court.

Two other main parts of Moody Gardens include Moody Gardens Hotel and Palm Beach. The hotel has 303 luxury rooms, an exotic swimming pool, casual and fine dining, a spa, full-service salon, fitness center, and more. In Palm Beach you'll splash in cool lagoons and waterfalls or tan on a tropical white sandy beach surrounded by palm trees. Also enjoy a visit to Dockside Café & Jacuzzi and a trip down the Yellow Submarine/Octopus waterslide.

Moody Gardens sea view. © Elaine L. Galit, 2000.

Keep in mind that the busiest months are April and May. In the year 2000 they had as many as 2-3,000 children a day for the educational programs. We recommend that you do not plan your visit for any mornings in April and May. Instead, consider scheduling your trip in the fall when they have more flexibility, fewer programs, and smaller crowds. You and your child will have a better overall experience visiting the exhibits and have more accessibility to the staff who are there to answer questions and enhance your learning and enjoyment.

What doesn't get mentioned enough about Moody Gardens are the two unique therapy programs established by the Moody Foundation in 1982. Hope Therapy is the cornerstone of Moody Gardens and inspires the disabled, aids the injured and elderly, and has changed the lives of thousands of people since its inception. The development of Moody Gardens was inspired by Foundation Trustee Robert L. Moody's son, who sustained a head injury in an automobile accident and who subsequently discovered the miraculous healing powers of animal-assisted therapy. An outreach program was added where smaller animals are taken to nursing homes, shelters, and hospitals. In addition, Hope Therapy expanded to include horticulture therapy, through which individuals with disabilities could improve sensory awareness and motor abilities.

Moody Gardens is a nonprofit educational facility dedicated to using nature for the advancement of rehabilitation, conservation, recreation, and research. Too often these major contributions by Moody Gardens are forgotten, but they are an essential cornerstone of the complex.

The admission fees, membership fees, and donations support their strong education, conservation, and research efforts. The Moody Foundation of Galveston funds them. Group rates for the general public are available. Call in advance for details and fees. In addition, there are field trip programs with a focus on education that may be of interest to special groups such as college level students or an organization like a dive club. They are flexible. Call the education department to discuss possibilities.

Rainforest Pyramid

A World of Wonders!
One Hope Boulevard, Galveston, Texas 77554

Ph: 800-582-4673
Fax: 409-744-1631
Web site: www.moodygardens.com
Attraction tickets available at all ticket booths. There are various plans available, including a Day Pass. Ticket booths open at 9:30 a.m. Call ahead for pricing.
Summer Hours: Open daily from 10 a.m. – 9 p.m.
Winter Hours: Sun. – Thurs. 10 a.m. – 6 p.m.
Fri. – Sat. 10 a.m. – 8 p.m.
Closed December 25th
Last admission one hour before closing

Amenities: include lockers, strollers, and wheelchairs. First aid and diaper changing facilities are provided. Gift shop and dining services available. Membership passes may be purchased that provide unlimited free admission and special members only events for one year.

Surprise: Large parrots can have a biting force of 700 pounds per square inch, so don't upset them and don't get too close.

Rainforest Pyramid at Moody Gardens. "Three macaws." © Vikk Simmons, 2000.

Children love the *Butterfly Hatching Hut,* the *Bat Cave,* and the *Insectarium.* Flamingos strut down pathways, parrots sit on perches, spreading their feathers, and orchids bloom throughout. Children are fascinated with the bold colors. Bats hang from the cave ceiling, and fruit kabobs abound. The butterflies are released twice a day at 11 a.m. and 2 p.m.

Rainforest Pyramid at Moody Gardens "Turn a path and watch the flamingos strut."
© Elaine L. Galit, 2000.

Another major attraction is the main fishpond containing *huge* fish from the Amazon basin. Take advantage of the many benches throughout the rainforest and enjoy the cascading waterfalls, exotic plants, animals, and butterflies as they captivate your senses.

The Rainforest is an AZA (American Zoo and Aquarium Association) accredited facility. This means they must meet very demanding criteria as far as the care of the animals and the educational value and content the complex provides. This one-acre rainforest, sitting within a 10-story glass pyramid, showcases exotic flora and fauna of Asia, Africa, and the Americas.

Do's and Don'ts

- *Do* take advantage of the Moody Gardens staff. They are there to answer questions and help you and the children have a more enriched experience.

- *Don't* touch the animals. Talk to your children in advance and remind them that the animals aren't pets. "Remember," says Kelly Drinnen, Education Curator, "anything that has a mouth can bite."

- *Do* look for the question and answer cards. If you can't find anyone to answer a question or if the person doesn't know the answer, you can fill out the postcard with your personal information and your question. The staff will find the answer and mail the card to you.

Does your child have a birthday coming up? How about a *Wild Things* party at the Rainforest? Parties include a decorated party area, a themed birthday cake, refreshments, a loot bag for each child attending, 24 coordinating invitations, and a visit to the Rainforest. Party is limited to 2 hours. Attraction attendance may extend beyond party time. (Other parties are *Wet 'n' Wild* at the Aquarium and *Beach Bash* at Palm Beach. Call for details.)

Education Programs for Groups

Call 800-582-4673 or 409-744-4673 Ext. 4332 for information and reservations. They have a number of packages, including combinations, and a variety of fee schedules depending on the arrangement you select. (This applies to all pyramid programs.)

> *Note:* Field trips are essentially school groups and have a minimum requirement of 20 participants, including adults. The plan is open to public schools, home schools, and the general public. The focus of the programs is on kids, so they require a specific but limited number of chaperones (adults) per program. Home school groups operate under the same guidelines as school groups. Check the general group rates for families as well as general groups of adults and children.

Moody Gardens offers a number of educational programs including outreach and educator programs, field trips designed for specific grade levels, as well as special events created specifically for scouts, overnight adventures, kids camps, birthdays, and star parties. Call for details on the *Good Grades Program* that allows A/B honor roll students free admission to one Moody Garden attraction. Special camps are held during spring break, too.

> *Tip: The Education Department has produced an excellent Tropical Rainforests teaching guide full of information and activities that can provide greater understanding of what rainforests are and why they are important. A great bargain for $10 and available to teachers, home schoolers, and the general public.*

The Education Department is terrific. Kelly Drinnen, Education Curator, and her staff provide a well-rounded program that includes events for educators, home schoolers, and the general public. A member of the staff is on hand during the twice-daily butterfly releases to answer any questions. The multidisciplined programs and materials have been annotated to the Texas Central Knowledge and Skills. Rainforest programs include the highly successful outreach program *Traveling Rainforest Trunk* that creates a total sensory experience with animals, indigenous music, intriguing artifacts, fragrant spices, medicinal plants, and traditional clothing. A new *Rainforest Exploration* field trip program allows children to have hands-on fun with exotic animals at The Learning Place followed by a self-guided exploration of the Rainforest. They'll visit a tropical "classroom." Field trips are available for grades K-12. An annual Open House is held for educators.

> *Tip:* Call for the comprehensive Education Program Brochure, which details the programs above and the Pyramid Kid Camps (day camps and sleepover camps), summer camps, as well as special Scout Programs and Overnight Adventures. You'll also receive information on the birthday party packages.

Reservations are required for all education programs at least two weeks in advance and are taken on a first-come, first-served basis. Adult chaperones are required to accompany groups at all times and must remain with their group. Groups are welcome to bring their lunches or make reservations for the lunch packages available. Call for information on programs designed for educators. Be sure to ask about the teacher planning passes.

Aquarium Pyramid

A World of Wonders!
One Hope Boulevard, Galveston, Texas 77554

Ph: 800-582-4673
Fax: 409-744-1631
Web site: www.moodygardens.com
Fees: Attraction tickets available at all ticket booths. There are various plans available, including Day Passes. Ticket booths open at 9:30 a.m. Membership passes that provide unlimited free admission and members-only events for one year are available.
Summer Hours: Open daily from 10 a.m. – 9 p.m.

Winter Hours: Sun. – Thurs. 10 a.m. – 6 p.m.
Fri. – Sat. 10 a.m. – 8 p.m.
Closed December 25th
Last admission one hour before closing

> ***Tip:*** *Ask for the Moody Gardens Map & Guide brochure.*

Amenities: lockers, strollers, and wheelchairs, first aid and diaper changing facilities, gift shop and dining services.

> *Note:* For more detailed information on Moody Gardens Pyramid attractions, go to the Rainforest Pyramid and the Discovery Pyramid entries.

Explore the depths of some of the world's oceans in the Aquarium Pyramid. The North Pacific, South Pacific, South Atlantic Oceans, and Caribbean Sea are all featured. Giant glass viewing areas display marine life; 130,000 square feet and 1.5 million gallons of water house more than 10,000 marine animals. Visitors explore these waters without getting wet and enjoy everything from

Aquarium Pyramid at Moody Gardens. © Vikk Simmons, 2000.

tuxedo-clad penguins to sharks, stingrays, and thousands of colorful fish. Stop by the Ports of Call food court and the Aquarium Gift Shop, watch daily dive presentations, visit the touch tanks, and walk through the Ocean View Room.

Playful seals frolic on rocky shores and dive below the surface of cold, pristine water. Over 200 species of colorful native fish swim in, out, and around coral reefs and greet visitors in the South Pacific exhibit.

Children love the king penguins. They watch the penguins and copy their waddling walk; they have their photographs taken with the penguins lined up in the background. A favorite remembrance of the Aquarium is a copy of king penguin art. Each penguin, an artist in his own right, has produced his own work of art. You'll delight at the individual penguin's expression of art made by their footfall. The museum's gift shop has framed prints and various replicas of their art.

Moody Gardens "Tuxedo-clad penguins in Aquarium Pyramid." © Elaine L. Galit, 2000.

"The Aquarium is unique in its offering of extraordinary underwater views, touch tanks, tide pools, and guest-to-diver communications to create the ultimate underwater classroom," said Dr. Vanoy, lab director and curator of fishes. Ever wanted to know what it was like to dive underwater? Take a walk through the one-million-gallon walk-through tunnel. You'll feel like a diver surrounded by sharks, reef fishes, snappers, eels, sea basses, and other marine life.

Education Programs for Groups

Call 800-582-4673 or 409-744-4673 Ext. 4332
for information and reservations.

Fun and exciting camps, overnights, and outreach programs are offered year round. Education programs include an annual Open House for educators, Exploration Combinations, Fundays, and a wonderful *Night on the Reef* Overnight Adventure. In the field trip program *Ocean Exploration*, your child will dive into the depths of ocean life and visit an "underwater" classroom. Special pyramid kids' camps and summer camps allow for children to discover what lurks underneath the ocean waves or explore a lush, tropical rainforest. Be sure to call for details on the *Good Grades Program* that allows A/B honor roll students free admission to one Moody Gardens attraction.

Reservations are required for all education programs at least two weeks in advance and are taken on a first-come, first-served basis. Adult chaperones are required to accompany groups at all times. Groups are welcome to bring their lunches or make reservations for the lunch packages available. Call for information on programs designed for educators.

Other Listings

Armand Bayou Nature Center (ABNC)

8500 Bay Area Boulevard
P.O. Box 58828, Houston, Texas 77258

Ph: 281-474-2551

Fees: Children 4 and under Free   Children 5-17 $1
       Adults $2.50   Seniors (60+) $1
       Members Free

Hours: Tues. – Sat.   9 a.m. – 5 p.m.
        Sunday   Noon – 5 p.m.
        Closed on Mondays

Note: The ABNC web page has a new address! Please update your bookmarks with the following: http://www.abnc.org.

The bison are coming!...

Armand Bayou Nature Center (ABNC) is a private, not-for-profit wildlife refuge and wilderness preserve. ABNC is the recipient of the Lone Star Land Steward Award (sponsored by the Texas Parks & Wildlife Department), which recognizes excellence in wildlife habitat management and conservation on private lands.

ABNC's mission is to provide environmental education and to preserve and manage the ecosystems it protects. ABNC is one of only four Texas State Coastal Preserves and one of the last bayous in the Houston area not channelized. It protects 2,500 acres of remnant ecosystems, including wetlands, riparian hardwood forests, and a coastal tall grass prairie.

Children will marvel at more than 370 species of birds, mammals, reptiles, and amphibians including white-tailed deer, armadillo, swamp rabbit, bobcat, coyote, poisonous and nonpoisonous snakes, turtles, alligators, and frogs. The chirping sounds of birds such as warblers, flycatchers, orioles, and painted buntings fill the air, only to be punctuated by the cry of birds-of-prey such as osprey, owls, and kites. Over 220 species of birds rely on the Nature Center Preserve as a safe resting place during their long migratory journeys.

In addition to over 1,500 acres of wetland habitat, Armand Bayou includes one of the nation's few native prairie preserves. It is the largest urban wildlife preserve in America and perhaps the world.

Tips:

- Children love bugs, and there will be plenty of chances for them to encounter insects who make the center their home. It's a good idea to use some insect repellent before you arrive.

- The insects play an invaluable role as predators and prey in the circle of life, so no swatting, please.

- The center provides special programs including *Spring and Fall Migratory Bird Weekends,* an annual *Earth Day Celebration, Creepy Crawlers Halloween Event, Children's EcoCamps, Farm Day Weekends, Winter Adventure for Children,* a monthly *Wildlife Focus Special Events* and more.

- Guided tours are available throughout the year, as are *Dawn/ Dusk/Night Wildlife Observation Walks.* Please call the nature center for schedules and reservations.

The bison, listed earlier, will soon have a new enclosure. ABNC is also working on many additional children's educational programs, so be sure to check the web site or call for further information on this constantly growing nature preserve.

Bayou Wildlife Park

5050 FM 517, Alvin, Texas 77511

Ph: 281-337-6376

Fees: March – August:

Adults – $8.95   Children (3 -12) – $5.50 Under 3 – free

August – March:
Adults – $7.95   Children (3 -12) – $5   Under 3 – free

Hours: March – October: 10 a.m. – 4 p.m. daily
November – February: 10 a.m. – 3 p.m. daily
September – February: Closed Mondays
(Subject to closing during inclement weather)

Looking for a great way to let your child learn to care about the animals in our midst? Let them wander through some of the eighty-six acres of prairies and woods filled with free-roaming exotic wildlife and birds. Animal lovers are able to see and feed animals from all over the world.

Visitors will find a jeep-pulled tram, petting zoo, children's barnyard, gift shop, and restrooms. While no food is available, there are picnic areas.

Tips:

- The tram ride runs about every 20 minutes and lasts approximately 40 minutes.

- Strollers are not needed outside of the main barnyard.

- Buckets of animal food may be purchased at the entrance for $2.

- Remember to take sunscreen and insect repellent.

For a great educational adventure, especially for pre-K and kindergarten classes, be sure to go on "a wildlife safari" at Bayou Wildlife Park. Students can experience how deer, giraffes, ostriches, zebras, camels, alligators, and many other animals live in the wild. They will also enjoy feeding the animals by hand while learning the importance of taking care of wild animals. While exploring the farm animal petting area, children can observe how mother goats feed their babies.

Big Boggy National Wildlife Refuge (Big Boggy NWR)

Brazoria National Wildlife Refuge Complex
1212 North Velasco, Suite 200
Angleton, Texas 77515

Ph: 979-849-6062
Web sites: http://southwest.fws.gov
http://www.gorp.com/gorp/resource/us_nwr/tx_big.b.htm

Although Big Boggy NWR is closed to the public, the refuge does invite specially arranged tours and maintains a public waterfowl-hunting program. Volunteers and staff teach an outdoor class providing the students with hands-on experience.

The refuge is an important part of the Great Texas Coastal Birding Trail and from November through February is alive with more than 100,000 waterfowl and sandhill cranes returning to their winter homes in the coastal salt marshes.

Blue Barn Fun Farm

Hwy. 359, 3/4 mile on 1458
37103 FM 1458, Pattison, Texas 77466

Ph: 281-375-6669
Fees: $6 per person   Groups of 20+ $5
Reservations required. Open year round.
Hours: Mon. – Fri.   10 a.m. – 2 p.m.
Saturday   10 a.m. – 3 p.m.
Sunday   1 p.m. – 5 p.m.
Amenities: There are barnyard animals, playground/picnic area, and food services. Restrooms available.

For an entertaining and appealing way to teach children about farm animals, take the kids to explore this family farm. More than a petting zoo, it's a hand-on learning experience. Enjoy a tour of this 30-acre facility as you and the children learn the basics of farm animals and how each item on a farm can be used to make a living.

The children are allowed to milk a cow, fish for crawdads, and learn the proper way to handle a host of farm animals from bullfrogs to emus, bunnies to turkeys. Before they can feed the sheep, the children are taught how to grind up the corn, just as people did in times past.

Tips:

● Pumpkins are available in October and November. Seed plantings are given out in the spring.

● Call ahead for reservations, as groups of 10 are needed for the tour. Individual families will be grouped together.

● A restroom break is recommended before taking the hayride since the playground only has an "old-fashioned" outhouse.

● Birthday party packages available.

● Don't forget sunscreen, insect repellent, and a camera.

Carol's Country Place

1923 Trammel-Fresno Road, Fresno, Texas 77545

Ph: 281-431-2664
Fax: 281-431-1309
Weekdays: Adults/Children - $5.35 Under 18 months - $2.70
Weekend: Adults/Children - $6.50 Under 18 months - $3.25
Check for group pricing. Families welcome.
Reservations required.
Hours: Weekdays: 8 a.m. – 5 p.m. (flexible)
Weekends: 10 a.m. – 1 p.m. and 2 p.m. – 5 p.m.
(5 p.m. – 8 p.m. on request)
Amenities: Restrooms are available.

Take an educational as well as exciting trip. Students will have a good time learning at this family farm that emphasizes education with lots of hands-on fun. Some of the activities include feeding the cows, ducks, and geese; taking a hayride along a spooky path; milking a cow; touring the hen house; petting small animals, such as rabbits and goats; taking buggy rides; slipping down a giant hayloft slide; and enjoying face painting.

There's also a guided farm and garden tour, nature walk (for older kids), picnic and play area, and gift shop. Birthday party packages are available.

The *Meet the Critter* presentation allows children to touch small cuddly animals like Rose, the prairie dog and Sonic, the hedgehog or Cookie, the opossum. Special events include Easter egg hunts in the spring, water play games, cane pole fishing, free snow cones in the summer, and a visit from Santa Claus during the winter holidays.

Tips:

● Don't forget the sunscreen and sack lunch.

● Take the camera for those special moments.

● Consider using bug repellent.

J-Mar Farms

Calfee Road, Conroe, Texas

Ph: 800-636-8595
Fees: Adults $6   Children (2-12) $5.50   Under 2 Free
Hours: Open daily 9:00 a.m. – 6:00 p.m.
Amenities: Restrooms available

J-Mar Farms bills itself as an educational petting farm. With more than 200 animals and guided tours offered, the children have an opportunity to get close and feed the animals.

The petting farm, with more than twenty different types of animals, offers children the opportunity to view animals in many different ways. Parrots, rabbits, pigs, pheasants, deer, and goats greet the children, and don't forget to see Elmer, the 1,000-pound pig, Piquito, the trick horse, and, would you believe, fainting goats? A pony ride is also available.

Other features include a swing, hay barn, play area, two-person paddle boats, and an Indian village. Activities offered include cane pole fishing, lake fishing (no fee), hayrides, tent camping, and picnicking in the pavilion. A bed and breakfast and birthday parties are also available.

Mercer Arboretum

22306 Aldine Westfield, Humble, Texas 77338-1071

Ph: 281-443-8731
Fax: 281-443-6073
Hours: Winter 8:00 a.m. – 5:00 p.m. daily
       Summer 8:00 a.m. – 7:00 p.m. Mon. – Sat.
            10:00 a.m. – 7:00 p.m. Sunday
Fees: Members are free
Membership: Individual $15 Family $25 Student/Senior $10

Tip: *Spring is the best time to experience the gardens.*

Horticulture abounds at Mercer Arboretum, containing Houston's largest display of native and cultivated plants. Visitors enjoy the sensory experience and view many different plant collections: gingers, perennials, ferns, tropicals, bamboo, Louisiana iris, and daylilies. Identification is easy as all plants have signage. Trails lead the visitor through many types of gardens and collections including the Arboretum, Butterfly and Display Garden, Herb, Herbarium, Maze, Native Plant, Perennial, Research, Rose, Tropical, and Xeriscape gardens. Design elements include bridges, ponds, topiary designs, benches, gazebos, and many rest spots. Paths loop around bogs or ponds, and the long boardwalk through the Hickory Bog highlights the area's unique ecosystem.

The arboretum is a great outdoor classroom for any group, including schools. Reservations and a security deposit are required. Science and literature classes are offered the first Saturday of each month, with a professional storyteller reading a children's book or a local artisan illustrating the story. The children are then encouraged to participate in experiments and explorations of the plants mentioned in each story. Call for details.

Look for the *Summer Ecology Camp*, guided tours and self-guiding children's scavenger hunts, and a county branch library nearby. Annual events include Arbor Day tree giveaways, Earth Day celebrations, and a Critters Christmas Tree Party. Pack your camera, beware of poison ivy, especially on the west side, and remind children that picking plants is not allowed. Most trails are stroller-friendly.

Nature Discovery Center

7112 Newcastle, P.O. Box 777, Bellaire, Texas 77402-0777

Ph: 713-667-6550
Fax: 713-667-7654
Office Hours: 9:00 a.m. – 5:30 p.m.
Discovery Rooms Hours: Tues. – Sun. noon – 5:30 p.m.
   Classes are held in the mornings. Lectures, field trips, classes
   for adults and children are offered. Call for details.
Web site: www.naturediscoverycenter.org

> ***Tip:*** *Check out the Kids Page on the web site!*

If there is one thing we heard over and over while visiting various nature related facilities, it was praise for the Hana and Arthur Ginzbarg Nature Discovery Center. We urge you to visit their informative web site. The center offers classes for adults and children and is highly interactive. Also mentioned over and over were the Discovery Rooms. They are filled with exhibits, activities, live animals, and things to touch, and all are about life in the Texas

Gulf Coast area. Imagine your child touching a snake or peering into a microscope and seeing nature in its most minute form.

The center is a valuable resource and offers classes about nature and science to families, as well as offering exhibits, field trips, and outreach programs. Here are just a few: *Nature Storytime*, a free preschool drop-in program every Wednesday at 12:30; the new *Pollywog Patrol* for children ages 20-36 month; *Nature Detectives* for 3-to-5-year-olds; *Eco-Explorers* for 5-to-7-year-olds; and a variety of *Scout Programs* for Brownie, Junior, Bear, Wolf, and Webelos. Do go to the web site; do visit the center.

Workshops and classes are offered for teachers, and there is a Teacher's Corner on the web site. The *Nature at your Doorstep* classes meet TEKS standards. Field trips, special events, traveling exhibits, and more await the inquisitive.

The Texas Zoo

P.O. Box 69, 110 Memorial Dr., Victoria, Texas 77902

Ph: 512-573-7681

Fees: Free to children 12 and under; $1 for 13 and over.

Hours: Open daily, except for Thanksgiving, Christmas, and New Year's Day, from 9 a.m. – 5 p.m., and open until 6 p.m. from May to August.

E-mail: txzoo@viptx.net

Web site: www.viptx.net/texaszoo

Established in 1976 and located on seven acres in Riverside Park, the Texas Zoo is young and growing.

In 1984 the Texas Legislature, recognizing the zoo's unique concept and its contributions to wildlife conservation, honored them by proclaiming the Texas Zoo "The National Zoo of Texas."

The zoo's collection consists exclusively of animals indigenous to Texas and is the only zoo in the nation devoted entirely to showing and tending animals native to one particular state. The zoo's animals represent the ten different habitats that exist in

Texas. This is an opportunity for many to observe native Texas wildlife at close range.

Children will enjoy the "Zooboose," a railroad caboose that exhibits endangered animals. The staff at the Texas Zoo provides educational programs on various topics.

Toolbox Tips

Outfitting the Young Nature Explorer

If you want to encourage your child to explore nature's wonders, here are some items any child's home laboratory might contain. Most of these items can be found around the house or in toy stores, hobby shops, hardware stores, and some specialty nature stores: magnifying glass, binoculars 4x, flashlight, sketchpad and pencils, stopwatch, tweezers, eyedroppers, compass, bottles, jars, plastic containers, beakers, an inexpensive 10-gallon aquarium, spoons, insect net, prism, lenses, small mirrors, field guides, and an inexpensive or disposable camera.

Science in Action

If you have a backyard or a nearby field, you have a great lab for a child to explore. Rather than waiting for the school to push the science fairs, why not encourage your child to initiate his own scientific investigations. Potential science projects abound around the home. Here are a few to get you started:

● *Birding*—Your child can build his own birdhouse, or you can buy a birdhouse kit or an inexpensive bird feeder and put it up. An inexpensive field guide or a book on backyard birds from the bookstore or library can get your child started. Suggest that he or she keep a list of the birds and draw them. Another good idea is to keep a logbook and record everything that happens.

- *Gardening*—Buy a packet of seeds, the fast growing ones like pumpkin, radish, or bean. Let your children create their own special garden patch. If you don't have a yard, help them find an inexpensive container for the seeds that will allow the plant to fully grow. Suggest that your child keep a log of everything he or she does and observes so she can learn the plant's growing cycle.

- *Bugs and tadpoles*—Encourage your child to explore the outside. Talk about dragonflies, butterflies, bumblebees, frogs, tadpoles, and toads. Your child can catch a bug and put it in a jar with holes or a terrarium in order to feed, study, and make notes. Then the child will release the insect back into the wild. What can a child learn from watching ants? How many different kinds of frogs can your child identify in your backyard?

- *Butterflies and moths*—Go on a butterfly and moth hunt. Moths often fly around at night. Have your child turn on the back porch light and actually look at the moths. They're not just ugly, brown, and little. On a closer look, your child will find incredible patterns and colors. Create a butterfly habitat and attract butterflies by providing them with a few simple needs. If you want monarch butterflies to breed in your habitat, you must plant milkweed. A number of books describe the specific plants that provide nectar sources for adult butterflies. We've provided a list of books on butterflies and on butterfly gardening for the Houston area recommended by the Cockrell Center.

Best Time to See Wildlife

Early morning or dusk is the best time to see most animals. Many are *crepuscular*, meaning they are active at dawn and dusk when the light is changing. Rabbits, birds, and squirrels are some that you may see.

Butterflies

Do a little research on the monarch butterfly. Did you know that monarchs migrate through the Houston area in October? You might plant a small butterfly garden (in the ground or through container gardening) in anticipation of their migrations. Having a Butterfly Watch would be a great activity for late summer. Contact one of the biological supply houses and order butterfly larvae and habitat and watch a butterfly develop. Great fun! Keep a small notebook and write down your observations.

Craft Activity: Make butterflies out of tissue paper and wire or clear contact paper with sticky sides together. Use permanent color markers to color the butterflies and hang them from the ceiling.

How to Keep a Nature Journal

Have your child keep a nature journal. Natural scientists usually record the day, the time, even the weather when they make entries. Often sketches are drawn of the bird, the leaf, and the bug that caught their eye. The journal helps the child develop his observation skills.

Begin a Logbook

Every scientist maintains a logbook to track his or her experiments. Simple entries with the date, time, and the project named begin the entry. A description of what the child says, what happened, and what he or she learned may follow.

Tropical Rainforests and Oceans of the World

The Moody Gardens Education Department has produced several excellent teaching guides full of information and activities. Written to help students and teachers, each chapter has activities for K-5, grades 6-8, and grades 9-12. These can be used to prepare the child before a visit or to enhance the learning experience afterwards. *Tropical Rainforests* provides more of an understanding of what rainforests are and why they are important, while the *Oceans of the World* guide links the processes of the ocean with our everyday lives. These are excellent bargains at $10 not only for educators and home schoolers, but for those parents and grandparents who seek to expand the education and experience of the children in their lives. (There is another booklet offered called "Bats of the Rainforest," call for details.)

How to Make Slime

A simple mixture of Borax, Elmer's glue, and water in various proportions will produce great slime. Add a few drops of green food color to make it even grosser. The slime does not have to be refrigerated and will last for months. Great stuff to squish.

Butterfly Finger Puppets

Go to a local discount store and buy a bunch of work gloves. Cut off all the fingers for the base. Each child gets one finger. Using foam and sequins, cut out wings and feelers, then glue the embellishments onto the cloth finger.

Resources

Books and Magazines

101 Things Every Kid Should Know About Science, Samantha Beres and Arthur Friedman. This is a good reference book for kids in grades 4-7.

Natural Geographic World (National Geographic Society)—Every month your child will read about geography, adventure, wildlife, and science. For ages 4-8

Ranger Rick (National Wildlife Federation)—Great magazine with powerful photographs of the world of nature.

Nature At Your Doorstep: Real World Investigations for Primary Students, Carole G. Basile, Jennifer Gillespie-Malone, Fred Collins, illustrated by Sabra Booth.

Educators can share the wonders of nature with students while building basic scientific knowledge and skills. Chapters are based on specific subjects, and the book is well organized and easy to follow. A great resource for teachers, it contains reproducible worksheets. This book is offered for sale at the Nature Discovery center whose premise is "nature is a great educator for people of all ages."

For Information on Rainforests

Amazon Center for Environmental Education and Research (ACEER)

Ten Environs Park
Helena, AL 35080
Ph: 800-255-8206 or 205-428-1700 ext. 242
Fax: 205-428-1711
E-mail: aceer@ietravel.com
Web site: www.erri.psu.edu/web/aceer.htm

Earth Foundation
    1515 Mitchelldale, Suite B-11
    Houston, Texas 77092
    Ph: 800-566-6539 or 713-686-9453
    Fax: 713-686-6561
    E-mail: curiculum@earthfound.com
    Web site: www.earthfound.com

Supply Houses

Edmund Scientific
    101 East Gloucester Pike
    Barrington, NJ 08007
    Web site: www.edsci.com

Carolina Biological Supply Company
    2700 York Road
    Burlington, NC 27215
    Web site: www.carolina.com

General Books

Butterflies of Houston and Southeast Texas by J. Tveten and G. Tveten (highly recommended!)

Butterfly Gardening for the South by G. Ajilvski

Butterflies and Moths: A Golden Guide by R.T. Mitchell and H.S. Zim

Handbook for Butterfly Watchers by R. M. Pyle

The Butterfly Book: An Easy Guide to Butterfly Gardening, Identification, and Behavior by D. Stokes, L. Stokes, and E. Williams

Butterflies of the Night by J. Tveten and G. Tveten (fascinating new book on moths)

Extremely Weird Frogs by Sarah Lovett (fun and informative)

Extremely Weird Reptiles by Sarah Lovett (fun and informative)

Reptiles and Amphibians by Catherine Herbert Howell (Published by National Geographic, this book is a wonderful children's reference.)

General Web Sites

Discover Online
www.discover.com
Great site for middle grade and high school students

National Geographic for Kids
www.nationalgeographic.com/kids
A wonderful site that opens up the world

Smithsonian Magazine's Kids' Castle
www.kidscastle.si.edu
Great site for your child to go to when in need of answers

National Wildlife Federation
www.nwf.org

Nature Conservancy
www.tnc.org

World Wildlife Fund
www.wwf.org

Nature Conservation Web Sites for the Beginner

Houston Arboretum & Nature Center
www.neosoft.com/~arbor/index.html
Want to know what types of habitat you'll find at the arboretum? Try this site and print out the trail map.

Hummingbirds web resource
www.derived.com/hummers/
Questions on hummingbirds? This is the place. You'll find many links to other great sites about birds.

Houston Audubon Society

www.io.com/~pdhulce./audubon.html

Where are the nature sanctuaries in the Houston local area? Go to this site for the answers and a list of other online Audubon Societies and ecological groups.

The Nature Conservancy Texas Chapter

www.tnc.org/texas/

Find out how to help preserve the state's natural surroundings. There's a *Nature Chat*, plus you'll discover research opportunities and preserve regions in Texas.

Armand Bayou Nature Center

www.ghgcorp.com/abnc/

Lists the center's many programs and activities. Take a walk, ride on a pontoon boat, or learn about turn-of-the-century farming and more.

Birdwatching Dot Com

www.birdwatching.com/

Tons of info on birding including reviews of birding videos and software

Planet Wildlife

www.planetpets.simplenet.com/plntanim.htm

Want web sites? You'll find a list of web sites containing kid-friendly information. Great site, cool graphics and sounds, too.

Texas Wildflowers

www.numedia.tddc.net/wildflowers/Apage.html

There are many different kinds of wildflowers found throughout Texas all year.

Kids F.A.C.E.

www.kidsface.org/

Kids save the environment. Find out how. All kinds of activities.

Texas Parks & Wildlife
> www.tpwd.state.tx.us
> Find out about upcoming events. Lots of information about the different species that are at risk in Texas and what's being done to protect them.

Peterson Online
> www.petersononline.com
> For budding birders, this is the place. Search their database of birding knowledge. Rich site full of lists, events, online *Bird Watcher's Digest*, and many links for the best bird sites on the web.

Additional Nature and Conservation Related Web Sites

Audubon Societies:
> Texas Audubon Society
> www.audubon-tx.org/

> National Audubon Society
> www.audubon.org/

> Bird Watching and Conservation Groups:

Bird Source
> www.io.com/~pdhulce/

> Butterfly Sites:

The Butterfly Site
> www.mgfx.com/Butterfly/Resource/index.htm

Texas Monarch Watch
> www.mgfx.com/Butterfly/Resource/index.htm

> Ecological Collections:

Biodiversity and Biological Collections Web Server
> www.biodiversity.uno.edu/

Texas Wetlands Information Network
   www.glo.state.tx.us/wetnet/

Ecological Resources:

U.S. Long Term Ecological Research Network
   www.lternet.edu/

World Conservation Monitoring Centre
   www.wcmc.org.uk/

Endangered Species:

Attwater's Prairie Chicken
   www.zooweb.net/apc
   The Houston Zoo is breeding birds for restocking efforts at the
   Galveston Bay Prairie Preserve as well as the Attwater's Prairie
   Chicken National Wildlife Refuge.

Endangered Species in Texas
   www.mbgnet.mobot.org/MBGnet/enviro/danger/TX.htm

Forest Conservation Groups:

Trees for the Planet
   www.goodwoods.org/planet

Forests Forever
   www.forestsforever.org/

Forest Habitat Campaign
   www.audubon.org/campaign/fh/index.html

General Conservation Pages:

Student Conservation Association, Inc.
   www.sca-inc.org/

National Parks and Conservation Association
   www.npca.org/home/npca/

The Conservation Fund
   www.conservationfund.org/

Habitat Conservation Groups:

The Trust for Public Land
www.igc.apc.org/tpl/

Adopt-A-Wetland Program
www.sci.tamucc.edu/aawp/welcome.htm

National Wetlands Conservation Alliance
www.erols.com/wetlandg/

Kids Links:

Clean Air Commandos
www.cleanairkids.org/cleanairkids/

Kids for Conservation
www.dnr.state.il.us/nredu/kids/kids/htm

Landscape Links:

Natural Landscape Scenic Photography
www.hardemanphoto.com/bio.htm

Nature Centers:

Houston Arboretum & Nature Center
www.neosoft.com/~arbot/index.html

San Antonio Botanical Gardens
www.sabot.org/

Oceans:

Mote Marine Laboratory
www.actwin.com/fish/species/fish.msql
(great information and interactives)

www.geocities.com/RainForest/2298
(lots of information and a fish of the week)

www.jasonproject.org
(great for popular research)

www.webshot.com
(great photos)

Plants and Gardening:

The Woodlands Wildflowers
www.mmcinc.com/wildflowers/

Gardening in Houston
www.burger.com/garden.htm

Rainforest Conservation Groups:

Tropical Rainforest Coalition
www.rainforest.org/

Rainforest Foundation International
www.savetherest.org/

Rainforest Action Network
www.ran.org

Smithsonian Tropical Research Institute
www.si.edu/stri or www.stri.org

For additional links visit the Houston Arboretum's link page at
www.geocities.com/rainforest/andes/6249nature/html
.nature.html.

3

Where Fun Has No Boundaries!

Finding a blend of education and recreation is one of the more delicate modern balancing acts parents are faced with on a daily basis. It is possible for your child to relax and have fun while he or she learns. Physical fitness plays a part in every child's education as most kids learn better when they're physically fit. The Houston Parks and Recreation Department is one of the single best resources offered to Houston families. What you may not realize is the almost limitless choices available under their broad umbrella. One thing is certain, this department is designed to help you in your pursuit of fun.

Houston Parks and Recreation Department

2999 S. Wayside Drive, Houston, Texas 77023

Main Switchboard: 713-845-1000

Events (recording): 713-845-1111

Community Centers: 713-845-1019

Web site: www.houstonparks.org

Houston Recreation Passport: This program benefits frequent users of the park services, providing a 10 percent discount off zoo admission fees, program registrations, greens fees, and tennis center court rentals. Members also receive the monthly events calendar.

Citizen Response Center Helpline: 713-645-HELP (4357) This program is for needed repairs, maintenance, and other citizen concerns in Houston's parks and open spaces. All calls regarding safety hazards will take top priority. The helpline operates 24 hours a day, seven days a week, with an operator on duty 8 a.m. – 5 p.m., Monday through Friday. After hours and on weekends, calls are recorded on an answering machine and answered the next business day.

> **Tip:** *In Houston parks, the department's monthly calendar of events is well worth your time. Averaging twenty plus pages, it is distributed to libraries, teachers, and community centers. If you don't find one, call the department and request a copy.*

Photo courtesy Houston Parks and Recreation Department.

As the Parks Department says, "Like Texas, Houston is big—really big. Houston's park acreage is so vast that just one of its parks, Cullen Park, could contain the entire park systems of Atlanta, Miami, Pittsburgh, and Tampa *combined*." Cullen Park is the second largest city park in the country. Nationally renowned Hermann Park, a 445-acre oasis of culture, zoology, horticulture, and recreation is about five miles from downtown. This one park includes the Miller Outdoor Theatre, the Houston Zoo and Children's Zoo, the Garden Center, the Museum of Natural Science, a famous equestrian statue of Sam Houston, a reflection pool and lake, a nostalgic miniature railroad, and a golf course. The park hosts about six million visitors a year. Current renovations will expand the lake and build a boat facility, complete the reflection pool, plant trees and ground cover, rebuild the outdoor theater, create wetlands, replace the golf clubhouse, replace the current central parking area with multiple dispersed, smaller, shady lots, and increase the number of park entrances from three to fourteen to reduce congestion. This is a far cry from the early days of the city's public parks.

Created in 1916, the Department of Public Parks began with two facilities—Sam Houston Park and Hermann Park. Today the Houston Parks and Recreation Department manages 293 parks and more than 200 spaces, covering 20,000 acres. They have 58 community centers with 3 new centers scheduled to open in 2001. Many children and their parents rely on the after school and summer youth programs available at the community centers. Three tennis centers, 156 neighborhood tennis courts, 251 playgrounds, 43 swimming pools, and seven 18-hole golf courses are available to the public. There are 80 miles of nature or hike and bike trails with 27 miles of trails along six bayous.

There is more. The Houston Parks and Recreation Department is dedicated to providing limitless sports and leisure activities for the entire family, and most are free. A variety of youth sports programs are available from golf to baseball, soccer to bicycling, street hockey to flag football. Thousands participate in the aquatic programs. Parks range in size from small open areas to the sprawling acreage of Hermann and Memorial Parks. Care to take in the theater experience? Check out the Miller Outdoor Theatre, the only free open-air theater of its kind in the United States. Every performance during the March to November season is free.

Had enough? No, well visit the Houston Zoological Gardens and make a special trip to the new Children's Zoo. Attend a bike rodeo and learn about bicycle safety. Experience life in the fast lane and check out the track racing at Alkek Velodrome.

Looking for the ultimate playground? Visit the Playground for All Children in Hermann Park and enjoy a safe, yet challenging environment for children of all ages and abilities. Kids will love the Water Play Zone. Play baseball on the 1998 Baseball Field of the Year (awarded by the Texas Turfgrass Association) at the Andy Anderson Baseball Field in Memorial Park. Join the nearly 3.5 million users of Memorial Park's senic and well-lit Lieberman Jogging Trail. Jog along this 3-mile, crushed granite jogging trail that features an exercise station equipped with an outdoor shower, not to mention the drinking fountains (including two fountains for dogs).

For the true nature lovers, smell the roses at the Houston Garden Center, find serenity at the Japanese Garden in Hermann Park, or explore the rich wildlife of an urban nature sanctuary located on the western edge of Memorial Park. Finally, the Houston Parks and Recreation Department produces or sponsors hundreds of neighborhood festivals and citywide events each year. These include the annual Fourth of July celebrations, the Houston International Festival, and the Asian, Pan African, and Cinco de Mayo Festivals.

Community outreach includes a Speakers Bureau with department experts available to speak on a variety of topics ranging from recreational programs to park safety for your community and civic meetings or events. Park Advisory Councils (PAC) give citizens a voice in recreational programming and allow them to help coordinate such activities as special events, fund-raisers, cleanups and more. There are even PACs for youth. Facilities are available for various events such as soccer matches, birthday parties, or family reunions. For those of a volunteering spirit, the parks department has a strong volunteer program if you'd like to help with various recreational programs, special events, and other activities.

Remember, the one word the Parks Department loves best is the word "free." Free is the common denominator for everything they do. Programs are open to anyone within the Houston city limits.

Note: For a complete listing of all the city departments, youth programs, and the Parks Department's programs, request the "Mayor's Youth Programs and Services" booklet. A youth services directory of all the city's youth programs, the booklet contains a complete listing of the Parks Department's youth sports programs, after school programs, aquatic programs, and facilities of interest. Program descriptions and contact information provides an excellent resource for parents, teachers, and community leaders.

Playgrounds

The Houston Parks and Recreation Department maintains 251 playgrounds. Safety is uppermost in their minds. They have a Safe Equipment Team that goes on a rotating basis to all the playgrounds to make sure the bolts are secure, the equipment works, and the fall surface is safe.

Parks

Parks are open by ordinance 6 a.m. – 11 p.m. The majority do not allow alcohol or glass containers. You are expected to clean up after any sports or activities. "Parks are as clean as you keep them." Do not bring barbecue pits; only use those provided at the park. Some of the larger parks have softball and baseball fields and basketball courts. There are restroom facilities at all parks.

Tip: If you want to guarantee space at a park, call for a permit; otherwise, if someone else shows up with a permit, you will have to leave. There is a refundable deposit.

If you're planning on using the park for a family gathering, a party, or a company picnic, call the Parks Department and verify that the facility will be clean. They are on a 14-day cycle, and you could be planning a party the day before the maintenance is scheduled.

General Information

- Need a place to hold a soccer match, birthday party, or a family reunion? The Parks Department has a facility to meet your needs. Call the Permits and Reservation office at 713-845-1003.

- For information on neighborhood and community relations, Park Advisory Council (PAC) Meetings, call 713-845-1232. PACs were formed to act as a voice for community based programming to ensure that the needs and objectives of each park community are addressed effectively.

- To reserve ball fields, call 713-845-1206.

- Want to celebrate your child's birthday party at a community center? The Parks Department now offers children 12 and under *free* birthday party space. Space is available on a first-come, first-served basis (does not include food, decorations, party favors, etc.). Call your neighborhood community center to reserve a space.

- Houston has seven municipal golf courses. For information and fees, contact the Houston Golf Operations, 1001 E. Memorial Loop, Houston, Texas 77007 or call 713-867-0386.

- The purpose of the community centers is to have safe gathering places for the community and families.

- The ultimate goal of the Parks Department is to have 25.5 acres per 1,000 residents.

- The department encourages Boy Scouts, Girl Scouts, Eagle Scouts, and Gold Award Scouts to contact them if the group is looking to do a major project. They have many opportunities available.

- Thinking of planting trees? Need advice on trees? Call for the *Tree Planting Guide*.

- Call in May for the Powerpak that details all the summer programs. Look for it in the *Houston Chronicle*, too.

Did you know that:

- A bat culture lives under a bridge along Buffalo Bayou trail? Watch the supervised bat feedings.
- All parks are pet-friendly?
- The Memorial Park Golf Course is rated as one of the finest municipal golf courses in the nation by *Golf Digest Magazine?*
- All parks and esplanades are mowed and de-littered every 14 days?
- You can shape your own neighborhood park and community center by getting involved with the Park Advisory Council?
- The Alkek Velodrome provides free bicycle safety and skill classes and has hosted six national championships?
- Nearly 21,000 children of all ages registered for the recreational and competitive youth sports leagues in 1999?
- Three Houston Metropolitan Area Youth Soccer League players have advanced to the professional level?
- Youth sports teams brought home a host of honors at the U.S. Youth Games in 1999 including gold and silver medals for soccer and a bronze medal for tennis?
- Four city parks were honored by the American Society of Landscape Architects (ASLA): Hermann Park, Memorial Park, Allen Parkway/Buffalo Bayou, and Heights Boulevard and were recognized as national landmarks for outstanding landscape architecture?
- There are Adopt-an-Esplanade and Adopt-a-Park programs?
- An estimated 1 million spectators attended the Reliant Energy Power of Houston Celebration?
- The zoo has more than 1½ million visitors each year?
- The Zoo Crew summer program enables teens, ages 14-18, to participate in the daily running of the zoo each year?
- The zoo has a new koala exhibit?

- Urban Park Rangers patrol on foot, bicycle, and motorized vehicles and monitor trails, picnic areas, and pavilions, as well as promote visitor safety and proper use of the parks and facilities?

- 300+ free helmets were distributed at 12 bike rodeos in 1999?

- Hermann Park is a flagship park that nearly achieves a "one-stop-shopping" experience with the vast opportunities and facilities available? You can spend the entire day there.

Check out the Houston Arboretum and Nature Center in Memorial Park for guided or self-guided tours. In their Discovery Room, children get hands-on experience with plants and insect gardens and sensory gardens.

Parks Department Youth Programs

Sports Programs

In the year 2000, more than 6,400 young athletes participated in just the summer sports programs.

Most programs and equipment are provided free to the child, although they may not take the equipment home. The sports programs are geared for kids who are "couch potatoes." The idea is to introduce the sport to the child and give him an opportunity to do something physical rather than simply be idle. Opportunities are then available for those kids who exhibit high skill and interest levels. The objective is to try and help kids obtain college athletic scholarships. So far, fourteen have obtained golf scholarships at universities. Several went into the Olympic Development Program.

The department hopes to have kids play golf in the World Cup in 2010. The golf program includes a nine-hole golf course available strictly for children. This newest golf facility opened its doors to all junior golfers of all skill levels in the fall of 2000. The course is located in F. M. Law Park (8400 Mykawa Road, just west of Hobby Airport). The First Tee Junior Golf facility includes the nine-hole course, a lighted driving range, a putting green, chipping green, and learning center. It will serve as the headquarters for the Parks and Recreation Department's award-winning Houston Junior Golf program, headed by PGA professional Robert "Pro" Olson. This is a place where the kids won't have to compete with adults for the opportunity to play and will be able to learn the sport for free. Each child who goes through the program receives golf clubs to use, but they cannot take them home. The children are taught etiquette, self-discipline, and sportsmanship, and from that they gain self-respect and motivation to achieve. Junior golfers also have access to a newly donated golf library.

More than 9,000 children ages 7-18 have participated in the hugely successful program, which teed off in 1994. Before this program started, inner city children didn't have any place to learn golf. Now any child who wants to learn the game has the opportunity and at no cost to them.

Fiesta Food Market partners with the Parks Department as a major sponsor of the soccer program. They provide uniforms, money to offset travel, and referees. Each sport typically has some level of sponsorship that allows the department to subsidize the costs.

The baseball program is part of the *Reviving Baseball in Inner City* initiative, sponsored by Major League Baseball. It is a nationwide program that teaches kids the fundamentals of the sport. The Parks Department has participated in the World Series since its inception. Programs include *Youth Baseball, Softball, and T-Ball, Houston Aeros "Summer Sticks Street Hockey" Program, Houston Metropolitan Area Youth Soccer League, USA Junior Team Tennis, City of Houston Tennis Program, Sprite/Houston Youth Basketball League, Shell Houston Junior Golf Program, Shell Safe Cycling for Kids, Shell Youth Cycling League, Youth Football, Zina Garrison All Court Tennis Academy, Houston Youth Volleyball League,* and *Hershey's Track and Field Program.*

Memorial Park Baseball Field. Photo courtesy Houston Parks and Recreation Department.

The department tries to offer sports that middle schools and elementary schools do not offer. A child is exposed to a sport in physical education in school, but there are no formalized teams. The Parks Department offers competition and skills development, so when a child enters middle school, he can try out with confidence. They go further than the playground mentality; the Parks Department gives them coaching and technique. The ultimate goal is for the sports programs to be stepladders that move children into high school sports. For some, sports can be an avenue to college scholarships.

Aquatics Programs

There are 44 free municipal swimming pools open from Memorial Day through Labor Day. Pools are closed on Mondays, except for Memorial Day and Labor Day. Registration for *Water Babies and Toddlers*, preschoolers, and youth classes is one week prior to class. Competitive Swimming takes place in June. For more information or a map, call 713-845-1009. Classes include:

Water Babies and Toddlers—For babies ages 9-18 months and toddlers 18 months-3 years. This program for parents and young children teaches safety skills needed to help babies and toddlers in or around the water. City of Houston water safety specialists teach classes. A parent, guardian, or responsible adult must accompany the child into the water.

Learn-to-Swim Programs—Designed to improve youths' and adults' ability to safely participate in water recreation activities, this program offers free classes for beginner, intermediate, and advanced swimmers. For preschoolers ages 4-5 years and children ages 6 and older.

Competitive Swimming—This free 12-week summer program offers opportunities in competitive swimming. The session culminates with four swim meets, including the city championships. Must be 6 years and older and must have mastered Youth *Learn-to-Swim* skills.

Junior Lifeguard Program—This youth volunteer lifeguard program develops participants' interests and skills in becoming certified lifeguards. For youths ages 16 and older.

After-School Programs

FACET (Fitness, Awareness, Crafts, Esteem, Trips, and Tournaments)—The after-school programs are offered free at every community center Monday through Friday, 3 – 6 p.m. For ages 6-14, the program offers activities such as arts and crafts, sports events, and field trips.

Summer Programs

FunQuest—Includes instruction in arts and crafts, games, field trips to local parks attractions, physical fitness, and more.

Field Studies 101: Teacher Workshops and Student Field Trips

Friends of Hermann Park,
P.O. Box 541447, Houston, Texas 77254-1447
713-524-5876

Bayou Parkland Classroom, 6520½ Almeda Road
(newly opened)
713-795-0930

Friends of Hermann Park offers a unique field studies resource to teachers and students. This *free* program brings students in grades K-8 on teacher-led field trips to explore the woods, ponds, and wildflower meadows of the Bayou Parkland in Hermann Park. The new facility is designed to help children experience outdoor science. The program is an environmental science based curriculum aligned with Texas Essential Knowledge and Skills. (TEKS, mandated by the Texas Education Agency, are the requirements for what must be taught in each subject for every grade level.) Workshops are accredited by the Houston Independent School District and the Texas Environmental Education Advisory Committee for 3 hours of professional development.

A typical trip lasts 2-3 hours. At the site, a Friends of Hermann Park staff member distributes free field study supplies and answers questions about the activities. Teachers then lead their students through three different habitats. Students participate in activities including dip netting for aquatic insects, exploring a woodland habitat, and collecting terrestrial insects. Before or after their activities, classes are welcome to eat lunch at picnic tables under the shade of oak trees. Student field trips are scheduled in the spring and fall. Call for times and dates of Teacher Workshops and general information on the Field Studies 101 program.

Houston Zoological Gardens

Hermann Park, 1513 North MacGregor, Houston, Texas

Visitor Information (recording): 713-523-5888
Visitor Services: 713-284-8300
Fees: Adults $2.50   Senior Citizens $2
          Children (3-12 yrs.) $.50   Children under 2   Free
Hours: Open daily 10 a.m. – 6 p.m.

Looking for the number one rated kid-friendly facility? The Houston Zoo is *numero uno.* Covering more than 57 landscaped acres, the Houston Zoological Gardens includes nearly 5,500 animals with more than 800 species represented.

Tips:

- Top-rated kid-friendly facility with terrific educational programs
- Duck Lake Feeding—call and check the days and times for feeding the birds at Duck Lake.
- Be sure and stop by the Sea Star Touch Tank in the Brown Education Center.
- Check for the times of the Sea Lion Demonstration held at the McGovern Mammal Marina in the Zoological Gardens.

Educational Programs

Brown Education Center—This 15,000-square-foot center has classrooms and a 300-seat auditorium. The facility offers workshops for teachers and a variety of educational programs for children and adults.

West Zoo Entrance. Photo courtesy Houston Parks and Recreation Department.

Zoomobile—The Zoomobile visits schools, hospitals, nursing homes, libraries, and community events to discuss various topics ranging from career awareness to exotic animal care. The Zoomobile is also available for organizations such as the Boy Scouts and the Girl Scouts of America.

Classes—An exciting and varied array of group programs for all ages are available. Classes are arranged by grade and/or age. Programs include after school classes, after hours tours, overnights at the zoo, and summer and winter camps. The zoo also offers classes for children ages 2½ and up, families, and educators. Programs include hands-on activities and interaction with live animals. (Contact: Jon Meyer @ 713-284-8330.)

John P. McGovern Children's Zoo

For information call 713-284-8330

Want a highly interactive place to take your child? The new Children's Zoo ranks at the top. Replacing the former children's zoo that entertained animal lovers of all ages for thirty years, the new $6 million children's zoo reveals a world of discovery and a wonderful experience for kids. "Children not only learn about the animal kingdom but also experience unique natural environments and habitats," says Oliver B. Spellman Jr., director of the Houston Parks and Recreation Department.

Located in the Houston Zoo in Hermann Park, the new Children's Zoo features six ecosystems of Texas:

- *City*—Enter into specially designed gardens that attract songbirds, butterflies, hummingbirds, and other creatures.

- *Forest*—Take a woodland journey along a boardwalk through tree forts and visit forest dwelling animals including deer, porcupine, skunks, and raccoons.

- *Coast*—Visit the coastal wharf. From the pier, observe alligators, snapping turtles, and shore birds. Inside the "bait shop," marvel at jellyfish, sharks, and stingrays.

- *Prairie*—Go "underground" and pop up into acrylic domes for eye-to-eye encounters with prairie dogs.

- *Desert*—Pass under a starry sky and enter the bat cave, complete with stalactites and stalagmites. Meet tarantulas, snakes, owls, and other nocturnal animals.

- *Farm*—Come on in to an old-fashioned Texas barn, featuring a hatchery, duck pond, donkeys, pigs, and, of course, cows.

Children's Zoo Opening. Photo courtesy Houston Parks and Recreation Department.

Your child can come face to face with a prairie dog, watch alligators and otters swim underwater, touch a live stingray, visit a bat cave, even climb into the treetops of a Texas forest. The new Children's Zoo "will provide all ages with a history of our state and its animals and their natural habitats," said Jane Block, Special Funds Chair for Zoo Friends of Houston, Inc., the nonprofit group that coordinated fund raising for the project. "It will not only be a place of knowledge for Texas residents, but also a warehouse of information for our visitors from all over the world."

Three 900-square-foot pavilions are interspersed throughout the new zoo for purposes such as educational classes, sleepovers, and party rentals. There's also an amphitheater located near the entrance featuring a colorful butterfly-shaped roof. The Discover Center will be full of hands-on activities for children.

Miller Outdoor Theatre

Hermann Park, P.O. Box 1562, Houston, Texas 77251

For updated program information, call 713-284-8350.
All events are subject to change without notice.
Free and open to the public. No reserved tickets. Open seating on
the hill.

There are 1,582 seats under the canopy and spaces for 27 wheelchairs. Special arrangements can be made for handicapped seating
by calling the theater office at 713-284-8353.

Note: Listening devices are available for the hearing impaired at
the box office one hour prior to curtain time. A valid Texas
driver's license or state issued ID card is required for deposit.
Call for performances that are captioned for the hearing
impaired.

Miller Outdoor Theater Asian/American Festival.
Photo courtesy Houston Parks and Recreation Department.

This is one of the nation's finest free open-air theaters, featuring entertainment from spring through fall. Located on 7.25 acres with 1,582 pavilion seats, the theater has a seating capacity of up to 20,000 on the adjacent hilltop. The facility has a 60,000-square-foot pedestrian plaza, a raised dining terrace, an upgraded sound and lighting system, 80 additional restrooms, and a new multimedia modular stage for world-class performing arts.

While performances at Miller Outdoor Theatre are free, some require tickets to the seated area. Tickets are available on the day of performance between 11:30 a.m. and 1:00 p.m. at the Miller Theatre Box Office. Any tickets remaining are given out one hour before curtain. Tickets are limited to four per person.

The facility provides over 100 shows and productions each year. If you want to expose your children to the arts, this is a great place to start. If you're not sure whether your child is ready for the theater, the productions aimed for kids can test your child's "sitting-power," some of which last only 45 minutes. The season schedule for 2000 listed performances ranging from the Broadway musical *Oliver!* to the Houston Ballet, from the Houston Symphony to the music of Motown, and from the Houston Shakespearean Festival to magical folktales from Africa.

Please note the following:

- Lawn chairs are permitted on the Miller Theatre hill; however, they should be placed only on the left side (facing the stage) so patrons on blankets can also see.

- Refreshments and other supplies for picnics are available to purchase at the concessionaire in the evening.

- No smoking is permitted in the seated area beneath the canopy or in restrooms.

- No glass containers

- No audio or visual reproduction of any portion of a presentation at Miller Outdoor Theatre is permitted without expressed written consent of the City of Houston Parks and Recreation Department and the Miller Theatre Advisory Board, Inc.

Miller Outdoor Theatre Weekend Children's Series—On select Saturday and Sunday mornings during the regular season (March through October), free theatrical and musical performances are offered. These quality performances are both educational and entertaining and are designed especially for children, young people, and families. Performances usually begin at 11 a.m. and last no longer than 45 minutes to an hour. Request a season brochure with a complete listing of all day and evening performances.

Alkek Velodrome

Cullen Park, 19008 Saums Road, Houston, Texas

Ph: 281-578-0693

E-mail: Alkekvelodrome@cs.com

Fees:

General Riding	$2	Adult	$1	Youth
Season Passes	$60	Adult	$30	Youth
Track Bikes	$3	Adult	$3	Youth
Development Classes	$25	Adult	Free	Youth
Shell Youth Cycling Programs			Free	

Hours:

Monday	7 – 9 p.m.	Classes
Tuesday	5 – 9 p.m.	General Riding
Wednesday	7 – 9 p.m.	Classes
Thursday	5 – 9 p.m.	General Riding
Friday	6 – 10 p.m.	Friday Racing
Saturday	2 – 6 p.m.	Open Riding
	6 – 9 p.m.	Sprints/Special Events
Sunday	2 – 6 p.m.	Open Riding

(Hours are subject to change)

Tips: Track bikes for rent: There is a stable of 30 track bikes available in various sizes from 44 cm to 61 cm. Helmets are available and required while riding. An attendant is always on duty to help you. Expert instruction is available. Call the Velodrome office at 281-578-0693 to reserve your bike.

This is an Olympic standard bicycle arena, available for serious training and general recreational use. The Alkek Velodrome opened in 1986 for the U.S. Olympic Festival. This unique bicycle facility is 333.33 meters in length and is one of twenty velodromes in the United States. The velodrome has hosted many state, regional, and national events. The facility was the first to host a state championship for Master rides (over 30 years of age). There are regularly scheduled hours for recreational riding. Whether for weekly workouts under the lights or just for fun, cyclists have a safe place to ride at the velodrome.

Visit the Velodrome—Designed as a one-day class, this program introduces clubs or other cycling groups to cycling on the track. The facility provides an experienced instructor who will teach the basics of riding at this unique facility.

Development Cycling Classes—These classes teach individuals the fundamentals of track riding for the beginning racer. Material covered includes general riding skills, pacelines, time trials, and sprinting. Classes are taught utilizing the facility's rental track bikes. Whether taking the first step toward a racing career or simply for recreational rewards, these classes are designed for people of all ages and abilities.

Friday Night Racing—The Friday Night Racing Series is designed to showcase the best tracking cyclists in fierce wheel-to-wheel racing. Sanctioned by the U.S. Cycling Federation, the series features a variety of events including points races, scratch races, Miss & Out races, unknown distance and more. Announcers keep spectators in the middle of the action. The Friday Night Races are divided into two seasons. The spring season begins in late March and continues until the Regional Track Competitions in June. The summer/fall season kicks off in early August and runs through the second Friday in October. Admission is free.

Saturday Night Races—The Saturday Night Races are designed for first-year racers, Pee Wees, who race in the infield of the Velodrome, and sprinters who compete in a round robin tournament.

Shell Safe Cycling for Kids—The class teaches children 4-12 years the basics of bicycle safety, riding, and technique. This one-session, one-hour free program teaches children the importance of bicycle safety in their neighborhoods. Children also participate in skills courses to hone their balance and bicycle handling. Children should bring their own bikes and helmets. Call to reserve a spot.

Shell Youth Cycling League—This is a four-week course for ages 10-16. Youths learn the basics of cycling during the first part of the program and then participate in a series of races. Riders compete using the track's bikes under supervision of an elite coach. The league has sessions in the spring and throughout the summer. Youths should bring their own helmets, or the track will provide free helmets for those who don't have them. The best riders in each session will qualify for the league finals in the fall when the best boy and best girl will win a free bicycle. This program is free. Graduates of the Shell Youth Cycling League are invited to participate in the Shell Select Junior Cycling Team at the Alkek Velodrome.

Playground for All Children

Hermann Park, 6001 Fannin, Houston, Texas

Ph: 713-284-1997
Hours: Daily 10 a.m. – 6 p.m.

A safe, yet challenging environment for children of all ages and abilities, this innovative playground is the flagship of Houston's park system. The 8-acre playground is nestled under large oak and pine trees. It features a Water Play Zone with timed spray elements on a blue rubber surface. In-ground sprays, poles, palm trees, and a spiral provide a variety of water effects for children to run through. An elevated water table containing two inches of water spills over into areas to create water play opportunities for the wheelchair bound or for those who must remain dry. A birthday party pavilion, patterned after the park's historic picnic pavilion, anchors the playground.

Hike and Bike Trails

The park system has 79 miles of trails
(nature, jogging, & hike/bike)

- 5 miles of self-guided trails introduce Houston Arboretum and Nature Center visitors to a pine and mixed hardwood forest, a re-created Gulf Coast prairie, ponds, and a native wildflower garden.

- Jog along Memorial Park's lighted 3-mile scenic, crushed granite jogging trail, one of the most heavily used trails in Houston.

- Mountain bicycles, with their fat, knobby tires and high torque gearing, can use Memorial Park's network of sanctioned, marked forest bike trails.

Other Listings

Bear Creek Park

16601 Clay Road, Houston, Texas

Ph: Park Office   281-496-2177
        Golf Club   281-859-8188
Hours: Unless otherwise noted, parks are open 6 a.m. – 11 p.m.

Your children will love to play where the bison roam in this park containing so many diverse activities. Bear Creek Park covers 2,000 acres, so there are plenty of picnic spots, play areas, tennis courts, and nature trails. There's even a small wildlife habitat with the following:

109

- A duck pond—where the public is allowed to feed mallard, Muscovy, and Peking ducks and geese.

- An aviary—where pigeons, doves, and a variety of parrots are housed near the pond.

- A Bird of Prey Exhibit—where hawks and owls hang out.

- A Prairie Dog Exhibit—where the life of this busy animal is depicted.

Other park dwellers are bison, ostrich, deer, sheep and goats, and a pot-bellied pig, and all create the perfect place to introduce your small child to a variety of animals in a natural setting.

No reservations are needed for the baseball, softball, and soccer fields or the tennis and horseshoe courts. You'll find a par three 18-hole golf course, too.

Bear Creek Park History—Shortly after Texas gained statehood in the late 1840s, early settlers arrived in this area around Bear Creek.

The community of Addicks, on what is now I-10, developed when the MK&T Railroad (Missouri, Kansas and Texas) came through in the early 1890s. The town was named for the first postmaster, Heinrich Addicks.

After torrential rains on the Buffalo Bayou watershed in 1935 caused serious flooding in downtown Houston, Houstonians prevailed upon Congress to authorize measures to control the runoff from the farmlands west of the city. The Addicks Reservoir was completed in 1948.

Harris County leased the land for what is now Bear Creek Park from the federal government in 1965.

Challenger Seven Memorial Park

2301 NASA Blvd., Clear Lake, Texas

Ph: 281-961-6881

> **Tip:** *Although a nicely maintained park near the Armand Bayou Nature Center, watch for mud during the rainy season.*

This park is dedicated to the memory of the seven astronauts who died on the space shuttle *Challenger*. Playgrounds and lookout points dot the trail toward a plaque in memory of the *Challenger*, then toward a boardwalk overlooking a large bayou.

Japanese Gardens (Hermann Park)

6001 Fannin St., Houston, Texas

Ph:	713-520-3283	Garden		
	713-526-0077	Golf Center		
Fees:	*Garden*			
	Adults	$1.50	Seniors	$1
	Children (3-12)	$.25	Under 3	Free
	Miniature Golf $2.00			
Hours:	*Japanese Gardens*			
	April – September	Daily	10:00 a.m. – 6:00 p.m.	
	October – March	Daily	10:00 a.m. – 5:00 p.m.	

> **Tip:** *For a brush with a different culture, visit the Garden on the 2nd Saturday of the month for a tea ceremony held at the teahouse.*

Join others at this impressive Japanese garden that grows native plants with traditional Japanese garden structures. A waterfall, pond, and gazebo are placed near a path through the gardens. A great place for a quiet stroll after an eventful morning or afternoon at surrounding Herman Park with its playgrounds, fishing, paddle boats, duck feeding, and animal watching at the zoo.

Japanese Garden—Hermann Park.
Photo courtesy Houston Parks and Recreation Department.

Jesse H. Jones Park and Nature Center

20634 Kenswick Drive, Humble, Texas

Ph:　　281-446-8588
Web site: http://jjpv.homestead.com/
Admission is free
Hours: March – February　　8:00 a.m. – 6:00 p.m.
　　　　　Except for December & January　　8:00 a.m. – 5:00 p.m.
　　　　　Closed Thanksgiving, Christmas, and New Year's Day

> ***Tip:*** *For old-time family fun singing and storytelling, attend one of the Pioneer Campfires held each month.*

Great exploration awaits at this 225-acre nature park with its Nature Center and five miles of paved hiking trails. Step into the past; tour the re-created pioneer village, circa 1820s-1830s, located at Rosebud Hill Pioneer Homestead and Indian Village. Visit a cellar, blacksmith shop, and pioneer home, then follow the path to the Akokisa Indian village.

This area is especially eventful on Pioneer Day in the fall, Texas Heritage Day in the spring, and Pioneer Christmas in December. During these events volunteers dress up and give demonstrations of pioneer life, such as candle and bread making. The homestead and village are open on Wednesdays from 10:00 a.m. – 4:00 p.m. and Saturdays from 1:00 p.m. – 4:00 p.m. and to groups by advance reservation.

Wander through the Nature Center that contains some hands-on exhibits and collections of animals, both live and stuffed—"a touch and feel" display. During the springtime you can view bee activities in a glass case outside the Nature Center.

Nature Trails, a playground (also built for the physically handicapped, in addition, there is a separate area for 2-5-year-olds), a wooden tepee, and picnic areas are also located in Jesse H. Jones Park.

Classes: A variety of interesting activities are offered monthly on weekends, including a Jr. Naturalist Club for ages 7-13. Call for a monthly program flier. The Tadpoles Club is a series of four weekly programs that will introduce 3-4-year-olds to nature, using animals, crafts, puppets, stories, and short walks. This class is held on Wednesdays from 10:30 a.m. – 11:30 a.m. and 1:00 p.m. – 2:00 p.m. Reservations required.

Tip: Be sure to check out Summer Nature Camps.

Note: County parks in the Houston area are located in four different precincts. We've included some of the major parks found in various areas of the county. Call you local precinct or check their web site for the location of a county park near you.

We've also listed the great picnic spots alphabetically at the end.

"Precinct 2 has 35 park properties; 14 are equipped with playground areas ... I would have to say that Bay Area Park would be more kid friendly than any other park in our system. Bay Area Park has a huge play area, duck pond loaded with ducks, fishing areas, and boardwalk piers that go out into the bayou. There are ball fields, open play space areas, picnic facilities, and a canoe launch," stated Gilbert Smith, Precinct 2 Parks office.

George Bush Park

16756 Westheimer Pkwy., Houston, Texas

The federal government created the Barker and Addicks reservoirs in the 1940s to control flooding on Buffalo Bayou. While the Barker Reservoir covers 13,500 acres, George Bush Park only occupies about half of this area.

In 1880 the early settlers raised cattle on part of the property. The rest was divided into small farms. The farmers planted rice, but the crops were not successful so the farmers sold their properties to ranchers by the early 1900s. The Texas Western Narrow Gauge Railway Company ran trains between Houston and Sealy through what is now George Bush Park between 1870 and 1895. The community of Barker was established when the Missouri, Kansas and Texas Railroad laid tracks in the 1890s alongside what is now Interstate 10.

Harris County leased 5,400 acres of Barker Reservoir for park purposes in 1982 and an additional 2,400 acres in 1987. The park was named Cullen Barker after the Cullen Foundation contributed money for the planning. As development of this park and the city's Cullen Park in the nearby Addicks Reservoir progressed and usage increased, the similarity of the two names caused confusion. For this reason, the Cullen Foundation agreed to renaming this park. Commissioner Steve Radack proposed the name George

Bush Park, and Harris County Commissioners Court approved the name January 28, 1997. This is the largest Harris County park.

Three picnic pavilions are available by reservation, in person, at the Precinct 3 Park Office. Deposits are required but returned upon compliance with rules.

Playing fields include nine soccer fields, five baseball fields, and one softball field. They are leased and maintained by players' clubs, but others can arrange to use them by calling the Precinct 3 office.

While the world-class shooting center is leased and maintained by the American Shooting Center, it is open to the public for a fee.

The Dick Scobee memorial Model Airplane Field was named for the late commander of the space shuttle *Challenger*. It is leased and maintained by the Houston Area Model Council, Inc. It can be used only by model enthusiasts with appropriate liability insurance, members of the model council, and members of the Academy of Model Aeronautics. Anyone can view the flying models, however, and it is an exciting treat to watch them fly.

Mary Jo Peckham Park for All Children

5597 Gardenia, Katy, Texas

Ph: 281-391-4482

The pool and building were built in the 1980s and operated originally as Founders Family Center. Harris County eventually acquired the property. Harris County Precinct Three had been looking for a place to establish a park that could be used and enjoyed by all children regardless of their physical abilities. Mary Jo Pekham Park for All Children opened in November 1991. The name honors the memory of the late Mrs. Rufus Walter Peckham. Mrs. Peckham was widely known for her willingness to help anyone in need.

The large playground was especially designed for children unable to enjoy ordinary playground equipment. The park boasts this playground is one "for all children."

The indoor heated, handicapped-accessible Olympic-sized pool is also equipped with barrier free, fully functioning dressing rooms.

The Muscular Dystrophy Association, United Cerebral Palsy Association of Greater Houston, The Spring Branch Independent School District, and the Katy Independent School District contributed suggestions for the playground, which was designed by Mary Goldsby.

The pool may be reserved for special groups and instruction like The American Red Cross, Adapted Aquatics classes for children and adults with disabilities, and adult exercise programs including water aerobics, lap swimming, and water walking. Individual and group therapy sessions are available by reservation.

Park Features: Lighted walking trail, gazebo, fishing, approved organized overnight camping, indoor swimming pool, miniature golf course.

Terry Hershey Park and Hike and Bike Trail

15200 Memorial Drive @ Memorial Mews

For hiking and biking, some of the best trails on the west side are located at Terry Hershey Park. The Cardinal Trail Loop is .9 miles long. The Blue Jay Trail Loop is 1.25 miles. The Mockingbird Trail spanning from Hwy. 6 to Eldridge Parkway is 1.62 miles and is a great bike trail. The Eldridge Pkwy. to Dairy Ashford trail is 1.5 miles, the Dairy Ashford to Kirkwood trail is 1.1 miles, and the Extension Trail is .31 miles.

Along the trails you will find handicapped accessible drinking fountains, restrooms, telephones, a playground, gazebo, sundial, runner's shower, and doggie drinking fountain. All of Cardinal Trail and Blue Jay Trail are lighted.

Parking is available at the Quail Trail from Dairy Ashford, I-10, Katy Freeway at the Cardinal Trail, near the Molly Pryor Memorial Orchard, and at State Highway 6 at the spillway.

Park Features: Picnic & BBQ, playground, lighted walking trail, hike & bike trail, exercise station, gazebo.

Favorite Picnic Parks

Bell Park

4800 Montrose, Houston, Texas

The quiet walkways, bridges, beautiful fountains and plant life are an oasis in the busy Museum District. Take a break and visit this park just north of Hermann Park off Montrose Boulevard.

Cullen Park

19008 Saums, Houston, Texas

Boasting more than 10,000 acres to explore along with picnic shelters, hike-and-bike trails, and playgrounds galore. Head out west on I-10—it's well worth the drive!

Cullinan Park on Long Drive

6700 Long Drive, Houston, Texas

This park is a delightful blend of nature, picnic, and playground areas located just outside the 610 Loop on the city's southeast side.

Downtown Parks

Downtown Houston, Texas

Sam Houston, Hermann Square, Tranquility, Market Square, Jones, and Sesquicentennial are included. Each has its own unique features, including cool fountains, flower gardens, and benches. Perfect places to rest and enjoy a picnic lunch in the heart of downtown.

Haviland Park

11600 Haviland, Houston, Texas

With a large pavilion and lots of shade trees for resting under, it's the southwest side's perfect getaway.

Hermann Park

6001 Fannin, Houston, Texas

With the Houston Zoological Gardens, Miller Outdoor Theatre, Museum of Natural Science, Japanese Garden, and an 18-hole golf course, there's always something to do. If you just prefer a leisurely day in the park, there are several picnic pavilions and even a water playground for the kids.

Hidalgo Park

7000 Avenue Q, Houston, Texas

A lovely gazebo and attractive grounds make it an enjoyable spot on the city's east side. A youth sports field and playground keep the neighborhood kids coming back for more.

Jaycee Park

1300 Seamist, Houston, Texas

The unique pavilion here makes it a favorite for family and company picnics. The accompanying open space begs for a ballgame of any sort.

Memorial Park

6501 Memorial Drive, Houston, Texas

One of the city's most popular parks, and here's why. The picnic areas are gloriously shaded, and there are lots of activities for the sports enthusiast—jogging, golf, tennis, softball, biking, rollerblading, and swimming.

Milby Park

2001 Central, Houston, Texas

Showcases sprawling grounds, towering trees, and a spacious picnic pavilion right along the bayou for a fun family gathering or quiet lunch al fresco. Experience this gem at Old Galveston Road and Highway 225.

Moody Park

3725 Fulton, Houston, Texas

The quintessential park for an old-fashioned Sunday stroll. Enjoy winding walkways lined with traditional park benches, shaded picnic areas, and a beautifully refurbished gazebo.

River Oaks Park

3600 Locke Lane, Houston, Texas

There's so much shade at this park, you might miss it for the trees. The playgrounds are ideal for young children, while the picnic areas offer a perfect spot for a busy day.

Tanglewood Park

5801 Woodway, Houston, Texas

Nestled in the Galleria area on Woodway. Stop for a rest at the gazebo or play a game of tennis on one of two lighted courts.

 # Toolbox Tips

Dino-Track Fun

Great fun to have with friends. The idea is to create traced footprints using human feet of various types and sizes mimicking dinosaur fossil tracks that have been found.

- Get a big piece of butcher paper and lay it on the floor.
- Have one child pick a motion they'd like to do, walking, running, jumping, and as they do this in slow motion, trace their footprints.
- Have the next person do the same. Continue until the paper has at least 5 to 7 types of footprints with different motions on them.
- Choose one child who did not participate in the tracing and have him explain what each footprint's motion was and which came first, second, and so on. This can be a two-day activity. For a variation, this activity can also be done in sand.

Zoo Scavenger Hunt

Plan ahead and create a scavenger hunt list of items for the child to find and identify.

from the Parks Department

Houston Showstoppers—This is a free year-round program of baton and flag twirling, cheerleading, dance, drill team, and percussion. For ages 6-18. Kids receive instruction and are given the opportunity to perform at various public events, parades, etc.

 Resources

General Web Sites

Santa Clara Park-Kid's Page
   http://claraweb.co.santa-clara.ca.us/parks/kids.htm
   Interesting site with activities for kids. Find out about ladybug lore, meet animals who leave their tracks in county parks, and learn how to make casts of animal tracks and lots more.

Nature's Web!
   http://library.thinkquest.org/3627/
   A bridge between nature and the Internet, this site has a collection of the top 15 U.S. national parks for kids. Lots of facts and designed for kids and by kids.

Texas State Parks and Historic Sites
   www.tpwd.state.tx.us/park/parks.htm
   Find out about Texas state parks.

Texas Parks and Wildlife
   www.tpwd.state.tx.us
   Check out the kid's page, *Outdoor Kids Network*, with its coloring pages, games, and the Outdoor Kids Program. For more information, e-mail education@tpwd.state.tx.us or call 800-792-1112 Ext. 65.

Outdoor Kids is a Texas Parks and Wildlife program that encourages young people to experience firsthand the natural culture and recreational wonders that are Texas.

Dinosaurs

Dinosaur Valley State Park
http://www.tpwd.state.tx.us/park/dinosaur/dinosaur.htm
Located on the Paluxy River near Glen Rose, Texas. Contains some of the best-preserved dinosaur tracks in the world.

Zoos

The Electronic Zoo
http://netvet.wustl.edu/e-zoo.htm
Clickable Electronic Zoo Logo©. Fun site with all kinds of information about animals and resources.

National Zoo
http://natzoo.si.edu
Features live animal cams, online animal demonstrations, and more.

Wildlife Conservation Society Online
http://www.wcs.org
Take an online tour for fun and games.

4

Playgrounds of the Mind!

More than anything, museums are playgrounds of the imagination. They can transport you back to the past; they can bring early civilizations to life; they can nurture your creativity; they can stir a child's wonder. Who wouldn't want to enter through the portal of a large mouth and journey through the human body or march up to the fully assembled bones of a T-Rex? Or maybe throwing paint onto a canvass is more to your liking? Adventures await the hearty explorers.

Take a trip to Houston's popular Museum District and you'll find sea lions and Cezannes, ancient tribes and contemporary artists, petrified dinosaur bones and a giant brain. Houston is rich in museum wealth. Not only are there museums in the District, they're tucked away in the Heights and planted across the street from the zoo. They spread from Galveston to Fort Bend County, and their subject matter is equally vast.

Art captures the imagination and ignites the senses. Taking a walk through a Texas-sized brain and staring out through a colossal eye provides an appreciation for the anatomy of the human body. Discovering your true weight on Mars or gazing up at the vast constellations in the sky blasts you into the world of astronomy and physics. Crazy art cars stimulate your creativity and tilt your perspective. Learning experiences abound in each and every museum for those who are willing to open their mind and their hearts to what awaits them.

Because many educators and school administrators don't seem to know about all the educational programs and exhibits available for children, the Houston Museum District for the past five years has held an annual Educators' Open House. Their idea is to show educators all the art, exhibitions, and programs that the museums offer.

Nine institutions including the C.G. Jung Education Center, the Children's Museum of Houston, the Contemporary Arts Museum, the Holocaust Museum Houston, the Houston

Museum of Natural Science, the Houston Zoo, the Museum of Fine Arts, the Museum of Health and Medical Science, and the Pioneer Memorial Log House hosted the last event in August 2000. This is a great way to reach out to children and to teachers and administrators.

Note: most museums do not allow photography indoors. Ask. If they do, they may not want you to use a flash; try 800-film speed.

Houston Museum of Natural Science

Permanent Exhibit Halls
One Hermann Circle Drive, Houston, Texas 77030

Ph: 713-639-4629
IMAX Show times: 713-639-IMAX (show times vary)
Web site: www.hmns.org (*good web site!*)
Purchase tickets and pay for parking at the Box Office. Purchase in advance by calling 713-639-4629.

Museum Fees:	Adult	$5	Child (3-11)	$3
	Members	Free	Seniors (62+)	$3
	Groups of 20+	$3 each		
IMAX Fees:	Adult	$6.50	Child (3-11)	$4.50
	Members	$4	Seniors (62+)	$4.50
	Groups of 20+	$4.50 each		
IMAX Double:	Adults	$12	Child (3-11)	$8.50
	Members	$7.50	Seniors (62+)	$8.50
	Groups of 20+	$8.50 each		

Garage Parking: $2 per car
Hours: Permanent Exhibit Halls
               Mon. - Sat.   9 a.m. – 6 p.m.
               Sunday   11 a.m. – 6 p.m.
        Wortham IMAX Theatre – Hourly shows
               Mon. – Thurs. 10 a.m. – 8 p.m.

Fri. – Sat.	10 a.m. – 10 p.m.
Sunday	11 a.m. – 8 p.m.

Museum Gift Shops/Collector's Shop

Mon. – Sat.	9 a.m. – 6 p.m.
Sunday	11 a.m. – 6 p.m.

Discovery Shop

Mon. – Sat.	9 a.m. – 8 p.m.
Sunday	11 a.m. – 6 p.m.

McDonald's Restaurant—located on the Main Level. Food & drink allowed in the restaurant and Grand Entry Hall only. Group lunches are available with advance purchase.

Mon. – Thurs.	9 am – 8 p.m.
Fri. – Sat.	8:30 a.m. – 11 p.m.
Sunday	10:30 a.m. – 8 p.m.

Museum Membership

Members enjoy special benefits including free admission into museum exhibit halls and gift shop discounts. Join at the Membership Desk in the Cullen Grand Entry Hall or call the membership office at 713-639-4618 or 713-639-4617.

Amenities: include elevators, wheelchair access, restrooms, baby changing stations, mother's lounge, and water fountains.

Museum Services Desk

The museum offers services for visitors with disabilities, nursing mothers, and those with special needs, including wheelchairs and many audio-described tours.

Tips:

- The web site is excellent and a great place to start to plan your visit to the museum. There are easy-to-follow directions from all areas of the city.

- For information on the Planetarium, Challenger Learning Center, Cockrell Butterfly Center, and Insect Zoo, see the Blast into Space and Bugs, Bats, and Butterflies sections.

- For information about captioning, ASL interpreters, audio descriptions, and other options call 713-639-4629 or 713-639-4687 (TTY) or visit the Museum Services Desk.
- Want more? Volunteer to work in any area of the museum from interpreting exhibits to essential behind-the-scenes jobs. Call 713-639-4643 weekdays.

The Museum is a vast place located on four levels. If your child loves rocks, the Mineralogy exhibit is a wondrous place to see rare

Collection Hall of Gems and Minerals.
Photo courtesy Houston Museum of Natural Science.

Paleontology Hall.
Photo courtesy Houston Museum of Natural Science.

and beautiful specimens. Or stare up at a T-Rex in Paleontology Hall. Take a stroll into the past and see a prehistoric Ice Age mastodon fossil. 3.5 billion years of life await you. Or maybe you'd enjoy seeing a 35-foot giant squid model in Strake Hall. Check out the Weather Center and discover the "magic" of KHOU-TV's chief meteorologist, Dr. Neil Frank, who does his "magic" of predicting the weather. Don't forget to try the six World WorkStations in the Earth Forum, an interactive multimedia learning experience in Earth geography, weather, history, and political patterns. Follow the path of energy from exploration to processing and delivery in the Wiess Energy Hall, and be sure you meet the museum's virtual docent in the Chemistry Hall. There's a fascinating world of interactive exhibits and computers.

Need a break? Take a load off and step into the world's premier IMAX theater with 400 seats and the finest motion picture system in existence. Can you imagine a giant 60- by 80-foot screen? You're guaranteed to "feel" the action.

The museum has a constant flow of breathtaking special events and exhibits that always bring a new world into view from historical sea voyages to Kremlin Gold. Ever wondered what it was like to live a thousand years ago or more? Experience early civilizations such as Aztec and Maya in the Hall of the Americas.

This is a place to learn and experience the wonders of the world. The museum more than meets its mission to educate with all the exciting array of educational programs available for children and adults. Classes, lectures, camps, workshops, field trips, and more fill participants with the thrill of discovery. And what member wouldn't want one of the special museum birthday parties?

The Children's Museum

1500 Binz in the Museum District

Ph: 713-522-1138

Web site: http://www/cmhouston.org

Fees: Tues. – Sat. 9 a.m. – 3 p.m. and Sunday noon – 3 p.m.
$5.00 per person   Seniors (65+) $4.00
Children under 2 and Museum Members Free
Daily 3 p.m. – 5 p.m.   Admission fee is $3
Free Family Nights   Thursday 5 p.m. – 8 p.m.

Groups: Group rate $4/person and 1 adult per 5 children
Group rate 15+, call 713-522-8185 for rates

Parking: $3 maximum with validated parking stub/$1 members

Hours: Tues. – Sat. 9 a.m. – 5 p.m.   Sunday noon – 5 p.m.
Closed on Mondays except for federal holidays.

Amenities: Wheelchair accessible and audio tours available

Tips:

- Have a two or three-year-old? Call for information on the *Time for Tots* program. Have an older three-to-four-year-old? Take advantage of *Preschool Pals* (adult accompanied). Fees are $24

129

for members and $30 for nonmembers for each of the three-session series.

- Call about the *Spotlight Performance*, which has a special activity included with the price of admission. Storytellers, musicians, magicians, and dancers perform in the 164-seat auditorium and entertain children every weekend as part of the Spotlight Performance series.

- If your toddler is a climber, then *Tot*Spot* is the place. Play in all forms awaits children 6 months to 3 years. Your child will love the Toddler's Castle, the climbing tower, and tunnel.

- Does your child fancy him or herself as the next Barbara Walters or Dan Rather? Kids strut their stuff on camera in the KID-TV Studio. Find out what television is like behind the scenes. Video cameras, props and costumes, storyboarding, even a sound booth help explain the world of television to your child.

- Want your child to learn a little economics? The Farm to Market Exhibit is the place to begin. Kids master banking and learn to shop. Weary parents can take time out at the Parent Care Café while the children work on a farm, milk a cow, and gather honey from a beehive and eggs from a chicken.

This is a kid-friendly museum and is most appropriate for children up to 12 years. With almost a half million visitors annually, the museum not only provides interactive exhibits but actual experiences in technology, history, culture, health, human development, and the arts. Want some good clean fun? Make a giant bubble and paint with bubble soap in the Exxon Bubble Lab. Wander through a greenhouse. Explore an Oaxacan village in Mexico and make tortillas, practice Spanish and Zapotec words, and "meet" the villagers through vivid photographs.

Maybe you have a child who wants to know how things work. Then How Does It Work, the Fondren Technikids Gallery is for you. Find out what happens when you turn on a car's ignition. Learn why magnets work. Find out about circuits, chemistry, and more. This completely hands-on exhibit answers a multitude of science questions. If that's not techno enough for you, navigate your way through the Cyber Clubhouse and experience an array of computer activities.

Perhaps your child is the artistic type. The open-air art studio will be the right spot to let your child be creative without worrying about being too messy. Easels with paint, clay, even computer art activities await. For those young wandering souls, the Red Caboose, an authentic 25-ton caboose, will help your little hobo-wannabe take pretend journeys almost anywhere while experiencing life on the railroad.

From the Babbling Bayou that encourages children to explore the world of water play to life in a Victorian Playhouse, the Children's Museum encourages fantasy play and hands-on experiences. Children can splash and launch their boats and play with water toys and games and then enter into pure whimsy in the fantasyland of the Victorian Playhouse.

The Museum of Fine Arts (MFA)

Every Sunday is a day for families!
1001 Bissonnet, Houston, Texas (between Montrose and Main)
P.O. Box 6826, Houston, Texas 77265-6826

Ph: 713-639-7300
Fax: 713-639-7707
Group Tour Office Ph: 713-639-7324
Web site: www.mfah.org
Fees:

Adults	$5	MFAH Members	Free
Children 5 and under	Free	Children 6-18 yrs.	$2.50
Students with I.D.	$2.50	Sr. Adults (65+)	$2.50
Glassell Students	Free		

Note: Certain exhibitions may require an additional admission charge.

MFAH Visitors Center and Parking Garage Hours:
Tues., Wed., Sat.	10 a.m. – 7 p.m.
Thurs. – Fri.	10 a.m. – 9 p.m.
Sunday	12:15 p.m. – 7 p.m.

Closed Monday (except for holidays)
Thursday is free thanks to Shell Oil Co. Foundation

Call for admission hours to the Audrey Jones Beck Building, the Caroline Wiess Law Building, the Lillie and Hugh Roy Cullen Sculpture Garden, the Glassell School of Art, the Glassell Junior School of Art, Rienzi, and the Bayou Bend Collection and Gardens.

> **Tip:** *Children 18 and under admitted free Saturday and Sunday with Houston Public Library Power Card or any other library card.*

Parking: Free in lots across from the museum on Bissonnet Street and north of Bissonnet off Main Street.

MFAH Membership: Enjoy free admission and other benefits

Accessibility: Wheelchairs are available on a first-come, first-served basis for all museum locations. Assistive listening devices can be reserved for tours, lectures, programs, and films. Call 713-639-7389.

Note to adults:

- Discuss with your child the importance of not touching works of art.

- Be sure to keep a safe distance from works of art at all times.

- Feel free to sit on the floor as you view and talk about works of art, but please do not lean on cases or walls in the museum.

Tips:

- *Museum Masterpieces:* The Do-It-Yourself Audio Tour is available in English and Spanish at the MFAH Visitors Center and in the lobbies of the Beck and Law Buildings. Fee is $5; $4 MFAH members.

The Audrey Jones Beck Building, the Museum of Fine Arts, Houston. Rafael Moneo, architect. Photo courtesy Houston Museum of Fine Arts.

- *Tours* (guided and self-guided), lectures, programs, and films are offered for student and adult groups. Tours are available to sight and hearing impaired visitors by appointment. Lectures, public programs, and family programs are offered year round.

- The Glassell Collection of African Gold is considered the best collection of 19th and 20th century African gold objects in the world.

- The new Beck Building connects by a unique tunnel (interesting neon light art) to the MFAH Visitors Center, which includes a full service ticketing and information center and a parking garage.

- Visit Café Express for lunch and/or dinner in the Beck Building.

If you have a child interested in the arts, the Museum of Fine Arts (MFAH) should be high on your list of places to visit. With wonderful programs geared for families, the museum has a constantly changing monthly program of fun, hands-on activities for the whole family. Make every Sunday an Art Sunday and participate in the Programs for Families. Choose drop-art activities, meet artists in residence, and attend story times.

Activities vary and in the past have included hands-on workshops in stained glass, creating a painting filled with bright colors and large shapes, or creating a jazzy collage. Sometimes you might create a clay teapot, or go on an art scavenger hunt through the museum.

> **Tip:** *Ask for the monthly Program for Families brochure or call for current activities.*

The sixth-largest art museum exhibition space in the country, the MFAH houses more than 40,000 works in all media. More than one million visitors tour the collections and exhibitions annually. The museum consists of two buildings, two art schools, two decorative arts centers, and an outdoor sculpture garden.

Educational Programs

The Glassell School of Art is the teaching wing of MFAH and offers creative opportunities for adults and children. The Junior School is the only facility in the country dedicated to art classes for children.

The Art Car Museum

140 Heights Blvd., Houston, Texas 77007

Ph: 713-861-5526
Web site: www.artcarmuseum.com
Admission: Free
Hours: Wednesdays – Sunday 11 a.m. – 6 p.m.

Art Car Museum interior (Galbe Delgado).
Photo courtesy Art Car Museum.

You've seen them on television every year promoting the Art Car Parade. Kids love 'em. They're those glorious art cars. Ever wondered what happens to them during the rest of the year? Well, some of those lovely, over-the-top, crazy, high-octane cars are parked at the Art Car Museum, a combination gallery and garage. If you want to jump-start an interest in art in a child or teen who never seems to cast an artistic glance anywhere, this may be just the thing. The museum doesn't have a bevy of educational tours or activities, but it's worth a visit for that special child.

In a metal building gleaming from scrap metal and chrome, this museum features works by artists Ron Hoover and Frank X. Tolbert II. You'll find the great beaded Cape buffalo head best-of-show 1997 *Faith*, a 1984 Camaro, and the 1967 Ford Galaxy known as *Big Red*.

Houston Maritime Museum

2204 Dorrington, Houston, Texas

Ph: 713-666-1910 – Call before you visit
Donations are encouraged. Call for group information.
Hours: Weekdays 10 a.m. – 5 p.m.
Weekend tours are available by appointment

We've included this small museum as a special place for a child who has an interest in model building. Located near the Medical Center, this museum opened at the end of 2000. At its heart is the "shipyard." Here you can see model ships built and restored. Some of the famous ships represented are the fastest passenger ships ever built, the SS *United States*, and a reproduction of the *Bounty* of "mutiny" fame.

Some of the ship models made at the Houston Maritime Museum.
Photo courtesy Houston Maritime Museum.

James L. Manzolillo, a retired naval architect, opened the museum to share his love and life's work. The diverse collection not only includes ships, but an 1812 diving helmet, a petrified tooth of a prehistoric shark, and a piece of coal salvaged from the *Titanic*.

If you have a child who might have a love for the ocean, who longs to sail the far waters of the open seas, or who is fascinated with models, this is the place to go. Mr. Manzolillo graciously and eagerly shares his knowledge of maritime science and history. He'll answer your questions. You're encouraged to linger and explore the small library.

The Museum of Health and Medical Science

1515 Hermann Drive, Houston, Texas 77004

Ph: 713-521-1515
Web site: www.mhms.org
Fees: Adults $4   Children $3
Hours: Tues. – Sat.   9 a.m. – 5 p.m.
         Sundays   noon – 5 p.m.
Group Tours and school field trips: Available by advance reservation. Group discounts are available for 15 or more.
Parking: Free and available in the front and back of the museum or on the street.
Health Hut: Area of vending machines with healthy snacks and drinks. Tables and chairs available.

Note: No outside food or beverages allowed.

Amenities: Restrooms and water fountains available.
The Amazing Body Store Gift Shop: Filled with health related books, T-shirts, games, and other gift items.

Each visit is a new experience. Child friendly, this museum focuses on science and health demonstrations with interactive family activities. Larger-than-life exhibits bring the human body into sharp focus.

Some of the activities and facilities include:

- *The Amazing Body Pavilion*—Enter through a gigantic mouth and begin a journey through the human body. Find out how the body works and how to keep it healthy. You'll sit on molars, teeth that would be the envy of any decent giant. The human pathway will show you the lungs, heart, kidneys, a Texas-sized brain, the ear, a giant eye, a bone show, and then the skin and

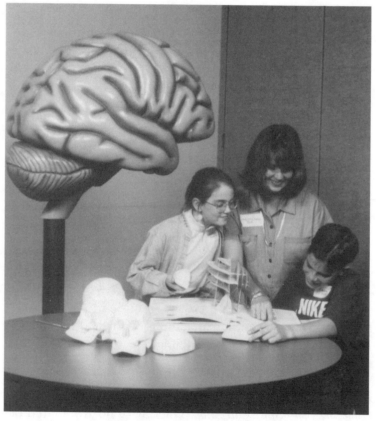

Museum of Health and Medical Science. The Brain.
Photo courtesy Museum of Health and Medical Science.

hand. The miracle of life is there for all to see. Along the way you'll find quizzing displays designed to lure you into learning more.

- *The Debakey Science Learning Center*—For 15 minutes every hour hands-on science classes engage visitors. Enter into these laboratory-styled classrooms and go through experiments led by volunteers and accompanied with visual aids. "Don't Sneeze On Me" is a sample topic.

- *Discovery Carts*—Located throughout the museum, these carts are quick to tease the children into hands-on demonstrations. These are manned by retired doctors or Baylor College of Medicine students.

- *Reception Room and Doctor's Garden*—Antique medical equipment decorates the reception room. Benches, flowers, even a sculptured water fountain enhance the Doctor's Garden. Relaxing and healthy.

Other Listings

Contemporary Arts Museum (CAM)

5216 Montrose Boulevard, Houston, Texas 77006

Ph: 713-284-8250
Fax: 713-284-8275
Web site: www.camh.org
Free admission
Hours: Tues. – Sat.   10 a.m. – 5 p.m.
       Thurs.   10 a.m. – 9 p.m.
       Sunday   12 noon – 5 p.m.
       Closed Mondays, Thanksgiving Day, Christmas Day, and New Year's Day.

Children needn't be enamored of art to enjoy the Contemporary Arts Museum (CAM). CAM presents major contemporary art exhibitions from both world renowned and regional artists as well as offering a range of programs for children and adults.

Contemporary Arts Museum.
Photo courtesy Contemporary Arts Museum.

A teacher whose class had visited the museum wrote, "Both docents explained the concepts behind these pieces so the students understood the artists' intentions—one of our class goals. One comment summed it up: 'Now it all makes sense.' When simple explanations elicit such a response you know you are all on target!" While many of the students have favorite exhibits, they will better understand "what is art?" after the philosophical and aesthetical discussions by the knowledgeable and interesting docents.

The Contemporary Arts Museum presents a variety of education programs. For more information about any of these resources, contact CAM's Department of Education and Public Programs. Some of the services offered are: Resources for Educators-Tours, Reserve a School Tour Online, Summer Institute, Resource Kits, Opportunities for Students-Career Information, Student Internships, Teen Council, Marian and Speros Martel Award, and the Cullen Foundation Education Resource Center Memorial Exhibition.

Galveston County Historical Museum

2219 Market St., Galveston, Texas

Ph: 409-766-2340
Fees: Free
Memorial Day to Labor Day: Mon. – Sat. 10 a.m. – 5 p.m.
                  Sunday Noon – 5 p.m.
Labor Day to Memorial Day: Mon. – Sat., 10 a.m. – 4 p.m.
                  Sunday Noon – 4 p.m.

Located in the 1919 City National Bank Building, the museum includes exhibits on the 1900 Storm; Native Americans during the time that Cabeza De Vaca occupied the Island in 1528; and the Galveston architecture of Nicholas Clayton. One of the really unique and historical features of this museum is a lighthouse lens and actual footage from the 1900 Storm taken by Thomas Edison's assistant.

Mardi Gras Museum

2309 Ships Mechanic Row, Galveston, Texas

Ph: 409-765-5930
Free self-guided tours
Hours: Weekdays 10 a.m. – 8 p.m.
       Saturday 10 a.m. – 10 p.m.
       Sunday 10 a.m. – 6 p.m.

The museum's focus is on Galveston's Mardi Gras festivities past and present. Costumes and historical memorabilia are on display as well as models of the street arches created for Mardi Gras.

Mardi Gras! Celebrating the Mardi Gras Museum.
Photo courtesy Galveston Park Board of Trustees. Photo by Lee Deforke Jr.

National Museum of Funeral History

415 Barren Springs Drive, Houston, Texas 77090

Ph: 281-876-3063
Fax: 281-876-4403
Web site: www.nmhf.org
Hours: Mon. – Fri.   10 a.m. – 4 p.m.
          Sat. – Sun.   Noon – 4 p.m.
Fees: Adults $6   Children 3-12 $3   Seniors 55+ $5

> **Tip:** *This is the country's largest display of funeral service memorabilia.*

Note: Some items children may enjoy seeing are the various cars and carriages, as well as some animal-shaped caskets. Give the museum a call before you rule them out.

Understandably the name of the museum might have you steer your youngsters away. However, before you turn the page, consider the history. One of the primary purposes of this museum is to preserve historical artifacts from the 19th and 20th centuries as well as to educate the public. And history is what your child will see. Some of the more fascinating items you'll find are exhibits and artifacts on a variety of political and celebrity figures. John F. Kennedy, Elvis Presley, Martin Luther King, Judy Garland, and John Wayne to name a few.

If cars are your thing, the museum boasts a collection of antique horse-drawn hearses and other one-of-a-kind vehicles still operable today. A full-size replica of King Tut's sarcophagus, Abraham Lincoln memorabilia, and exhibits of the Vietnam Wall Memorial and the Tomb of the Unknown Soldier are some of the other exhibits housed in this 20,000-square-foot museum.

The National Museum of Funeral History was founded not only for the purpose of preserving historical artifacts from the 19th and 20th centuries, but more importantly to encourage public education and enlightenment of our country's heritage of funeral service.

This museum has been nationally and internationally recognized and continues to change its exhibits and rotate its collections to make the experience different and interesting every time you visit.

National Museum of Funeral History. Examples of antique horse-drawn hearses.
© Vikk Simmons, 2001.

The Pasadena Historical Museum

201 Vince, Pasadena, Texas

Ph: 713-477-7237
Admission is free
Hours: Wed. – Fri.   9:30 a.m. – 2:30 p.m.
Sat.   9:30 a.m. – 5 p.m.
Sun.   1 a.m. – 5 p.m.

Note: Several sites nearby and adjacent to the museum are available for tour and visitation.

Throughout its history, Pasadena has borne several titles. It has been called the "Birthplace of Free Texas" because in 1836 Deaf Smith and his company of six men destroyed the bridge across Vince's Bayou and prevented the Mexican soldiers at the San Jacinto battlefield from receiving reinforcements or from escaping. This single act doubly assured the independence of Texas when the Mexican dictator Santa Anna was unable to find a way across the bayou as he fled from the battle. He was captured and prevented from returning to Mexico where he had planned to raise another army to subdue Texas.

The name "Pasadena" was given to the area by Colonel J. H. Burnett, a Galveston developer who laid out the town in 1893. He supposedly saw similarities between the climate and land in the area to that of Pasadena, California. The climate and the land, in turn, gave rise to the first economic mainstay of the area—farming. On 10- to 20-acre plots, strawberries, cantaloupes, figs, and Satsuma oranges provided a stable livelihood for its inhabitants.

Pasadena Historical Museum "Strawberry house."
© Elaine L. Galit, 2000.

Strawberries gave Pasadena yet another title—"Strawberry Capital of the World." Pasadena's strawberries became famous because of their size and sweetness and were shipped by rail as far north as Chicago and Kansas City where they brought premium prices. Twenty-eight train carloads a day left the Pasadena loading sheds. As the "industrial center of the south," Pasadena still pursues its destiny as the "Birthplace of Free Texas," as a town where work, family, education, religion, fun, and a healthy economy are the rightful inheritance of a free people who know where they came from.

For a day of history in Pasadena, start with a visit to the Parks House, adjacent to the museum. Admission is free to this nostalgic old farmhouse filled with 1920s furnishings built during Pasadena's early 1900s strawberry boom. Call or request a tour during museum hours.

Continuing down history's path, drive over to the Pomeroy Houses, at 202 and 204 Main Street. These houses were owned by an early Pasadena settler family. You can view business and domestic furnishings, the first city water well, and memorabilia from the 1930s to the 1950s. Admission is free.

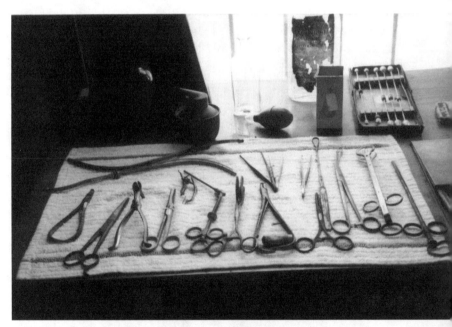

Pasadena Historical Museum "Ouch—Antique medical instruments."
© Elaine L. Galit, 2000.

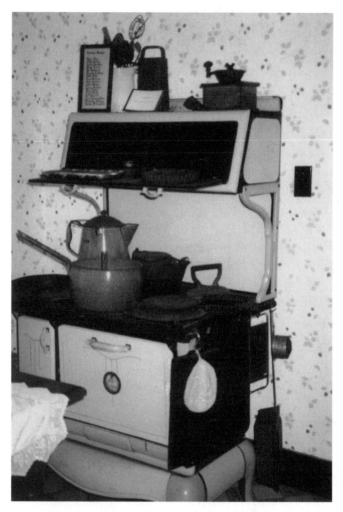

Pasadena Historical Museum "Antique kitchen stove."
© Elaine L. Galit, 2000.

Also nearby is Vince's Bridge, destroyed on April 21, 1836, by Deaf Smith and company thereby preventing Mexican army reinforcements from reaching the battle. On April 22, 1836, Santa Anna, commander of the Mexican army and dictator of Mexico was captured, assuring the success of the Texas revolution. The bridge is now on the grounds of the Simpson Paper Company.

Railroad Museum

123 Rosenberg Avenue, Galveston, Texas
(Rosenberg at Strand)

Ph: 409-765-5700
Fax: 409-763-0936
Web site: www.tamug.tamu.edu/rrmuseum
Fees: Adults 13-64 $5   Seniors 65+ $4.50
       Kids (4-12) $2.50   Kids under 4 free
       Group rates available
Hours: Summer 10 a.m. – 4 p.m. Daily
       Winter 10 a.m. – 4 p.m. Wednesday – Sunday
       Closed major holidays.
Museum gift shop
Amenities: Free parking is available at 21st St. and Santa Fe Place. Wheelchair accessible and smoke-free (smoking areas available).

Take your kids on a journey back in time inside one of the nation's most popular rail museums, the restored Galveston Union Depot. This is one of the largest train museums in the Southwest, containing more than 44 full-size railcars and locomotives.

Life-sized "ghosts of travelers past" fill the waiting room where you can actually listen in on their conversations. Located in a restored 1930s passenger depot, this museum exhibits an old waiting room, a model train layout of the port of Galveston, Pullman sleepers, cabooses, a diner car, a mail car, steam locomotives, and a new Railroad China display featuring plates, glasses, and silverware used in dining cars. You can also visit the museum's souvenir shop. A working miniature train is on display where children can view the train on the tracks at eye level, and exhibit-car displays encourage children to tap out Morse code and see a velocipede (handcar). Diesel and steam sounds as well as songs from the 1930s are heard.

The most impressive feature of Galveston Island's Railroad Museum is their Boy Scout program to earn the Railroading Merit Badge. The museum's web site has the details. Eagle Scouts who are interested in railroading may also sign up to restore an old rail car.

Galveston Railroad Museum.
Photo courtesy Galveston Convention & Visitors Bureau.

Tips:

- Unlike the exhibit cars, the railcars and locomotives are not climate controlled. They may get very warm in the Houston summer.

- Strollers may be difficult to maneuver in the tight quarters of the railcars.

- Outdoor seating with excellent scenery is available.

 Toolbox Tips

Before You Go

- Visit the museum's web site to find information on exhibitions or special shows. Find related books, articles, magazines, or other related web sites.

- Pick a well-known artist whose work will be seen and find a book about the artist's life or search the Web for information For example, Leonardo da Vinci was more than a great artist, he was an inventor and builder. Try to create an interest and provide the child with some advance information so he or she will see something more than a drawing on a wall. Help them learn about the artist.

- Search for books on scientists such as Marie Curié, Louis Pasteur, Albert Einstein, or Galileo. Think about what they did and why. What do you wonder about? Why? Are there things you want to make? Is there something you want to discover?

- What ancient civilizations might you see at the museum? Are you interested in the Incas? Do you know what happened to the Ananazi?

Follow-up

Create artwork that expresses feelings or emotions

When an artist creates a work of art that expresses how he feels or what depicts an emotion, the artwork is called *expressionist art*. Often artists use colors or shapes to create a feeling, such as using yellow for happy or a wavy line for a dreamy, soft emotion. Try to make your own:

1. Gather several sheets of paper and any kind of art materials such as colored pencils, paint, crayons, etc.
2. Now think of several emotions and draw a picture of how the emotion makes a person feel. How would you draw happy, angry, scared, sad? What about shy?
3. Consider how the color adds to the picture and the feeling. Warm colors are red, orange, yellow; cool colors are blue, green, and purple. Are you making lines that are strong and thick or thin and weak? Do the people smile, grin, or pout?
4. When you're finished, show the artwork to a family member or friend and see if they can guess which emotion you tried to re-create.

Art Postcard Story Starters

Pick out several art postcards from the museum and use them as story starters.

1. Look at the postcards and choose one to write about.
2. Create a short story from the art postcard.
   - Pick three items out of the card and use them to weave a story. For example, perhaps there is a dog, a little boy, and a lake. Why are they there? What is going on? What happens next?
   - Think about what the painting is trying to say, or write about how you feel when you look at the art.

- If the postcard has a person, what is that person doing? Why is he there? How is he feeling? What do you think is going to happen next?

The leg bone is connected to the thigh bone ...

Interest in anatomy can be fostered at any age. How many pre-schoolers know the old song of the leg bone connected to the thighbone, the thighbone connected to the hipbone, and on and on. Encourage your child to remember the song, and try to go through the entire body. Find a simple drawing of a skeleton to help.

- Draw the connecting bones of the leg, the foot, the arm, and the hand. Draw a complete skeleton, and try to name the major bones in the body. Color in the organs like the heart, the brain, and the kidneys.

- What do the different bones and organs do? Why do we have a hipbone? How many bones are in the foot? What is the longest bone in the body?

- Consider buying one of the anatomically correct skeletons that are made for children.

A log of museum trips

Talk to your child about the various museums and have her participate in developing a museum tour and plan the trips. Encourage your child to begin a logbook right away. Like any good tour guide, you'll want to decide which museum you'll visit first, second, and third. Go to the web sites. What is your child interested in? If your child is interested in space, plan a space odyssey.

- Pick three museums and decide the order of visits.

- Draw up a plan. What can you do before you go? Are there books to read? People to find out about? Web sites to gather more information?

- Write in the logbook the details of the plan.
- Visit the museums and make entries in the logbook during and after the visit. What did you see that you really enjoyed? What would you like to see again? Is there something else you'd like to do as a result of the visit?
- Consider taking a camera and photograph your child outside the museum.
- Take your favorite photographs and put them in the logbook and write a short entry about the photograph and what happened at the museum.
- Make a list of new things to do as a result of the visit.

Design Your Own Art Car

You've decided to design your own art car for the parade next year. What would your car look like?

1. Go through car magazines and find a picture of a car to decorate.
2. Think of a theme for the art car. Do you want to do a western car with longhorn horns on the hood and leather cowhide on the outside? Maybe you'd rather do an Easter car or a Christmas car? What about a cartoon car?
3. Make a drawing of your art car. Use crayons, colored pencils, paint. Cut out other pictures to decorate your car and paste them onto your drawing.
4. Name your car.

Trace Fossils—A great activity for several participants

> **Tip:** *Imprint fossils should be done with adult supervision.*

The purpose is to re-create a carbon imprint fossil. Gather a leaf, candle, paper, foil, and tweezers.

1. Burn the candle and hold the foil over it until there is a lot of soot built up. Use the tweezers to hold the foil.
2. Next push the leaf into the soot coating it as much as possible.
3. Place the leaf soot side down, and press it onto the paper without moving the leaf.
4. You get a great imprint fossil. The impression comes from carbon, although in real life the carbon comes from the plant itself and not the burning.

Model Building

Go to a hobby or model shop and pick out a new model to build. Do you want to build a ship or an airplane? See what other kinds of models are available. Pick one and build it.

Rock cycle

Tip: Should be done with adult supervision. For older children.

The purpose is to create examples of three types of sediment for comparison. Gather a mallet, 2 blocks of wood, crayon shavings, foil, candle, and a pie plate.

1. Examine the shavings. Explain that the shavings are sediment.
2. Next, put the shavings in a little foil packet and place between the blocks. Hammer gently; watch fingers. Explain that the blocks are heat and pressure provided by the earth.
3. Remove the foil and observe. Explain that this is now sedimentary rock. Compare the different sediments and note their differences and their similarities.
4. Place the foil back. Hammer again.
5. Remove. This now looks like metamorphic rock.

6. Stand the candle in the pie plate. Put the foil over the burning candle and hold with tweezers. Make sure that the sides of the foil packet are open. In time the crayon melts and leaks out. It may catch on fire but this is usually considered a highlight of the exercise rather than a bummer if it happens. It can smell.

7. The liquid crayon is like lava/magma depending on where it is in the earth.

8. Allow the liquid to cool. Note how this is indigenous rock. Have them return it to the sediment but crumbling it up as they do.

9. A good way to observe is to write with the "rock" each time. If possible make some identifications about the three types of rock and get samples. Have the child determine the type based on their concluded identification.

10. This is a good example of how a model works—or doesn't.

 # Resources

Books, Brochures, Magazines, and Information

Dinosaurs for Every Kid by Janice Van Cleave

Dragon Bones and Dinosaur Eggs: A Photobiography of Explorer Roy Chapman Andrews by Ann Bausom

The Body Book—Scholastic Professional Books Scholastic Inc.

The Big Beast Book: Dinosaurs and how they got that way by Jerry Booth

Related Web Sites

http://www.watchesuk.co.uk/dinosaurs
Dinosaurs Animated Graphics and Books—Animated dinosaur graphics and a large selection of book reviews

General Web Sites

Art Cars
> http://www/artcars.com/gallery/assem.html
> Images and information from the annual Art Car Parade in
> Houston, Texas. See what's been done in the past.

http://www.artcars.com/coverPC.html
> Photos of cars decorated with paint, toys, cameras, plastic
> junk, and other materials

Anatomy

You've seen the colossal eye and the giant brain, now you can find
out more about how they work.

Neuroscience for Kids Newsletter
> http://faculty.washington.edu/chudler/newslet.html
> If you like to read about ancient Egypt and have an interest in
> the brain, this is the newsletter for you (for ages 12+). It's
> informative. It's fun. Best of all it's *free*.

Neuroscience for Kids
> edu/chudler/chgames.html
> Games. Great site, very interactive. Games to learn about the
> nervous system and brain

Explorations 4 Kids
> http://www.gomilpitas.com/homeschooling/explore/Explore...
> A directory of web sites for learning

Neuroscience for Kids
> http://faculty.washington.edu/chudler/eyetr.html
> The Eye and Its Connections. Detailed lesson and lab experi-
> ment with teacher's guide, student guide, background
> concepts, related links, and references

Healthgate
> http://www3.healthgate.com/kthealth/index.asp

Kids' and Teens' Health, a comprehensive resource in article format for parents regarding their teen health-related issues and concerns

Dinosaurs

State of Wyoming
http://www.state.wy.us/kids.html
Kid's Page—The state of Wyoming's web page made especially for kids. Includes links to other web sites about the state, dinosaurs, the Wyoming Starbase Academy, and schools in Wyoming.

Wyoming Dinosaur Center
http://www.wyodino.org
Located in north central Wyoming and is known for some of the largest dinosaur fossil quarries in the world. Join staff paleontologists at a dig site in the field as they uncover large dinosaurs such as diplodocus, apatosaurus, allosaurus, and camarasaurus all from the Jurassic period.

4Dinosaurs
http://www.4dinosaurs.com
Includes dinosaur articles, resources, fun stuff, and links

Dinosauria On-Line
http://www.dinosauria.com
A tool for researching dinosaurs. Contains the Journal of Dinosaur Paleontology, a collection of essays and e-mail discussions whose topics range from what Archaeopteryx used its wings for, to evolution

Zoom Dinosaurs
http://www.zoomdinosaurs.com
Enchanted Learning Software—An online hypertext book about dinosaurs. Chapters include anatomy and behavior, extinction, fossils, and types of dinosaurs. Includes quizzes, dictionary, and classroom activities.

Dino Land
http://www.geocities.com/CapeCanaveral/Galaxy/8152
Interviews, news on recent fossil finds, virtual tours of famous sites and museums, and tribute to the great discoveries

Dinosaurs: Facts and Fiction
http://pubs.usgs.gov/gip/dinosaurs
Information from the U.S. Geological Survey

Dino Paradise
http://www.vcnet.toyama.toyama.jp/~saurs/sc_index.htm
For the dinosaur enthusiast, including information about dinosaurs, paleontology, and links to other sites

Wolfgang's Dinosaurs
http://members.chello.at/wolfgang.schwarz/dinosaurs.htm
Information on types of dinosaurs and misconceptions about dinosaurs. Includes extensive links to related sites

National Geographic
http://www.nationalgeographic.com/dinorama
National Geographic's links to dinosaur articles in *National Geographic* magazine

Dinosaur Illustrated Magazine
http://illustrissimus.virtualave.net/dimfront.html
Online magazine about dinosaurs

Model Building

Collecting Model Trains
http://kidscollecting.about.com/kids/kidscollecting/msu...
Links to sales and information sites if you want to make train collecting a hobby

Free-Flight Model Airplanes
http://www.luminet.net/~bkuhl/rubber.htm
This site supports free flight as an excellent hobby for kids or kids and parents together. Great beginner information.

5

Day Tripping!

for those times when you simply want to get away, consider taking a day trip. There are many places that are a short trek from central Houston, and a visit would be a great way for the family to spend a few hours together. These are fantastic places to travel back in time and relive the 1800s when Texas was first settled, or to sink into an adventure on the high seas by boarding the 1877 tall ship *ELISSA*.

Every year Texas students are given April 21 off to commemorate the fight for Texas independence and the Battle of San Jacinto. Every child learns Texas history. In Houston there are so many ways to bring the past alive. Be sure to take your child to the San Jacinto Battleground State Historical Complex and plan to spend the day. There are so many things to do, and it is easy to rediscover the past. Children scampering over the park area will find many historical markers depicting events of the battle.

If the 1800s are too distant a past, transport yourself and your family back to the days of the Great Generation and the war they won in the 1940s, World War II. With the release of *Saving Private Ryan*, children everywhere have shown an increasing interest in the happenings of World War II and its generation. It's easy to come face to face with a visit to the Battleship *Texas*. *Texas* was once the most powerful warship on the high seas; armed with 14-inch guns, she was feared for 32 years. In 1988 a major overhaul in dry dock began as part of a long-term restoration. The restoration continues, but the ship remains open and welcomes all visitors. This is a great time to actually walk on the ship that nations feared.

Did you know that:

- In 1835, on what is now the San Jacinto Battleground State Historical Park, General Sam Houston rallied his troops to battle, and eventually Texas independence, with the words "Remember the Alamo!"?

- The 570-foot San Jacinto Monument is listed in the Guinness Book of World Records as the tallest monument column in the world?

- The Battleship *Texas* saw action on D-Day in the allied invasion of North Africa and at Iwo Jima and Okinawa?

- 133,000 immigrants entered the Port of Galveston, once known as the "Ellis Island of the West?"

- The tall ship *ELISSA* is a floating National Historic Landmark and has been designated one of America's Treasures by the National Trust for Historic Preservation?

- Pirate Jean Lafitte made Galveston his base of operations in 1817 and called it Campeche? None of his legendary buried treasure has been found on the island—*yet*!

The Galveston Historical Foundation (GHF)

Our Past is in Your Future!
502 20th Street, Galveston, Texas 77550-2014

Ph: 409-765-7834
Fax: 409-765-7851
Education Programs: Lydia Miller at 409-765-7834, ext. 37 or
    e-mail: Lydia.Miller@galvestonhistory.org.
Web site: www.galvestonhistory.org

The Galveston Historical Foundation is Texas's oldest historic preservation organization. GHF membership includes a quarterly newsletter and free admission to all GHF operated properties as well as discounts.

GHF operates most of the museums in Galveston and offers a variety of educational programs including day camps and overnights. They are making a strong push in this direction so be sure to check out their web site. You'll find plenty of places to visit and things to do. If you or your child has an interest in the hurricane of 1900, be sure to watch the outstanding wide screen documentary *The Great Storm of 1900* at the Pier 21 Theater. You'll be transported back 100 years to Victorian Galveston when it was Texas's wealthiest city in the days before the hurricane. Then you'll witness the total devastation caused by deadliest disaster in United States history. For the pirates among you, watch the wide screen film *The Pirate Island of Jean Lafitte*. This pirate once called Galveston home, and the film chronicles his adventures.

Discovery Day Camps are adventures in history and part of GHF's summer educational program. The one-day camps are designed for children ages 8-10. Advance registration is required, and campers must bring a sack lunch and dress comfortably for outdoor activities. Previous history days have had campers use their imaginations to become pioneer children. They've played traditional pioneer games, made kites and gourd birdhouses, and learned to use a wooden spool knitter and card yarn. Still others have experienced a sailor's life and gone on a scavenger hunt on the tall ship *ELISSA*. They've sung the songs of chanteymen, practiced the basic knot tying of sailors, and tried other seagoing crafts. Still more have stepped into a Victorian fantasy. They've played croquet and parlor games and danced the Virginia reel. In high fashion they've participated in a 19th-century fashion show and ended the day with an afternoon tea.

Texas Seaport Museum & 1877 Tall Ship ELISSA

Pier 21 at Harborside Drive, Galveston, Texas 77550
Home of the *ELISSA*

Ph: 409-763-1877
Web site: www.galvestonhistory.org
Fees: Adults $6
          Students (7-18) $4
          Children under 6   Free
Hours: 10 a.m. – 5 p.m. daily
Discounts available for families and prearranged group tours.

Note: The *ELISSA* is not wheelchair accessible.

Here's a chance to find out what Galveston was like in the 19th century. Galveston's historic port has quite a history, and the museum has information in the computer database about more than 133,000 immigrants and their countries of origin, dates of arrival, and planned destinations.

Texas Seaport Museum. Photo courtesy of Galveston Historical Foundation.

Find out what life is like on the high seas with the exhibits "Life at Sea" and "Sounds of Sea" on the *ELISSA*. This beautiful tall ship is a wonderful place where children can actually touch history. The *ELISSA* is an iron barque and was built in Aberdeen,

Scotland, in 1877. She was restored by the Galveston Historical Foundation during 1976 through 1982 at a cost of $4 million. She is 205' long with 19 sails. Her original crew size was 12 to 13 and included 1 to 2 boys. That information alone is enough to fire the imagination of boys everywhere. Let your child scramble over the ship and imagine what it would be like to ride the seas on the *ELISSA*.

Educational Programs – Student Tour Information

Call 409-765-7834, ext. 37 for information or send email to Lydia.Miller@galvestonhistory.org

- *Tour 1*—Watch the documentary *Passage to Galveston: The Story of ELISSA*, the dramatic story of the tall ship's rescue and restoration. Then tour the *ELISSA* with a trained guide. Time: 60 minutes Cost: $2.50 per student.

- *Tour 2*—After viewing the documentary, students participate in a scavenger hunt that teaches them about the historic Port of Galveston. Students can also search for information about their ancestors in the museum's immigration database. They can see who entered the Port of Galveston, once known as the "Ellis Island of the West." Time: 90 minutes. Cost $2.50 per student.

- *It's a Sailor's Life*—An overnight program for young people. Opportunities abound for your child to experience this glorious time in history and spend a night on the tall ship. This is an opportunity that is easily worth more than its cost.

Imagine standing on the deck of the *ELISSA*. Cast your mind into the past and "remember" what it was like to feel salt spray on your face and to know the nature of the "square-riggers," those elegant tall ships of yore. During the course of the night you'll participate in the ancient art of knot tying, sing sea chanteys, and more. Sponsored by the Galveston Historical Foundation, this project is presented by the Texas Seaport Museum.

The program is for ages 8 and up with a minimum of 30 students, maximum of 40. There will be a minimum of one adult per five students. *Fee:*$35 per student. A $175 deposit is required. Held Friday or Saturday overnight from 6:30 p.m. to 9 a.m. Eat dinner before arrival, breakfast is served aboard ship. Call 409-763-1877 for dates and information.

The overnight program includes the following:

Set a Sail!—Tour the *ELISSA* and watch a special presentation of the wide screen *ELISSA, The Longest Voyage*. The novice overnight crew learns by doing, and they help set one of the huge staysails and work with the ship's volunteer crew to master seagoing knots and rope craft.

Set the Watch—During the night, the participants follow an old sea tradition and keep watch over *ELISSA* and the Galveston Harbor. Their young minds light up with visions of days when barques and brigs and full-rigged ships sailed into Galveston. They'll listen in the early morning hours to the wind caressing the rigging and singing of distant shores and times long past.

Set a Course! For Adventure—Education kicks in with teamwork, self-reliance, discipline, and plain, old-fashioned hard work. The participants will view exhibits and do on-site activities that will reinforce their history, science, and ecology knowledge.

Photo courtesy of Galveston Historical Foundation.

Sea Center Texas

300 Medical Drive,
Lake Jackson, Texas 77566

Ph: 979-292-0100
Web site: http://www.tpwd.state.tx.us/fish/hatch/seacenbr.htm
Fee: Admission free
Hours: Tues. – Fri.   9 a.m. – 4 p.m.
         Sat.   10 a.m. – 5 p.m.
         Sun.   1 p.m. – 4 p.m.

There is a small gift shop but there are no food services at the Center, so plan ahead with regard to lunches. Volunteers can provide directions to an area park for a picnic. A drinking fountain is near the restrooms.

The aquarium offers self-guided tours. Led by volunteers, hatchery tour times vary and reservations are required. Call ahead.

This is an interesting place to take children and offers them a chance to see up close the marine life of Texas bays and Gulf waters and conservation in action. Be aware, though, that the entire trip to the center will not take up a lot of time, so a planned picnic would be a good addition to this outing. Do take advantage of the volunteers who are there.

> *Tip: A catch & release pond is used during planned events. Kids get to catch and release the fish. Call ahead for dates.*

This one-of-a-kind marine fish hatchery has a 15,000-square-foot Visitors Center located on 75 acres in Lake Jackson, Texas. Tour the aquarium and see exhibits that picture life around a jetty, depict marshland, and house deep-water fish. The hatchery area contains an incubator holding "Mommy and Daddy" fish.

The center cost $13 million and opened in 1996. It is the largest red drum hatchery in the world and is serious business. The larvae produce stock for 36 acres of grow-out ponds where research is conducted on stressed fish stocks from Texas waters.

Sea Center Texas statue in front.
© Elaine L. Galit, 2000.

- *Touch pools*—Children love the shallow water touch pool. Blue crabs, hermit crabs, urchins, snails, anemones, and other marine animals become real to children when they are allowed to actually handle them. Don't worry, the pinchers have been removed. Your child will love the little shame-faced crab that spurts water like a fountain.

- *Salt Marsh*—Kids can actually see a section of coastal marsh as it is displayed in a long 1,000-gallon aquarium with a window more than 14 feet long. Natural debris covers a muddy floor dotted with oyster and clam shells. Fiddler crabs and shrimp entertain viewers. Shrimp, periwinkles, jellyfish, and other aquatic organisms are shown in their natural habitat.

- *Coastal Bay*—This 2,200-gallon aquarium houses species such as red drum, spotted sea trout, and snook over a sand, mud, and oyster reef bottom.

- *Jetty*—What child isn't fascinated with moray eels? This 5,000-gallon jetty exhibit nearly fills the entire back wall of the center. Granite blocks and boulders re-create a manmade jetty complete with moray eels. Barnacles, periwinkles, and other shelled animals encrust the wooden pilings. Rocks spill across the bottom while toadfish, groupers, black drums, and tarpon hover among the pilings.

- *Artificial Reef*—A big, green moray eel, the state's largest, greets children from inside this 50,000-gallon reef exhibit. Tripletails, pompano, and rockhind also tease viewers. Looking into this aquarium, you'll experience the only break in a seemingly end-less background that fades from the surf zone out toward the open Gulf.

- *Offshore Gulf of Mexico*—Your child will stare in amazement at Gorden, the 250-lb. grouper as he flaps his fins slowly and stares back. This 50,000-gallon Gulf of Mexico aquarium fea-tures red drum, blue runner, jack creballe, snapper, and others who stay out of the way of the 4-8 ft. sharks slowly circling over the crushed coral bottom.

- *Hatchery*—Though more suited for older children, smaller children do have a chance to see the baby fish if it's close to the release date. Children will enjoy seeing the broodfish tanks with windows that show the red drum fish and spotted sea trout.

- *Culture Ponds*—These thirty-five acres of fish culture ponds are used for growing larvae to 1-inch fingerlings. One half-acre pond is dedicated for special projects and research.

- *Marsh*—This exhibit shows children what elements are needed to create these brackish marshes. The area includes shallow ponds, fresh and saltwater marsh areas, and elevated walkways across the site complete with large decks for extended marsh viewing. Interpretive panels describe the habitats, aquatic animals, plants, and birds.

San Jacinto Battleground State Historical Complex

Located in Harris County, 22 miles east of downtown
Houston via Texas 225 and Texas 134
Web site: www.tpwd.state.tx.us

San Jacinto Battleground State Historical Park

Ph: 281-479-2431
Fee: Admission free
Hours: Open seven days a week
      March 1 – Oct. 31   8 a.m. – 9 p.m.
      November 1 – Feb.   8 a.m. – 7 p.m.

The battleground complex is the site of three grand historical sites: San Jacinto Battleground State Historical Park, San Jacinto

Museum of History, and the Battleship *Texas*. It is the site of the April 21, 1836 battle that won Texas independence from Mexico; home of the San Jacinto Monument, the San Jacinto Museum, and permanent berth of the historic Battleship *Texas*. In addition San Jacinto Battleground State Historical Park is 1,000 acres with picnic sites available.

Steeped in history, you'll find much to see and learn, but you'll also find time to relax, have fun, and enjoy picnics and barbecues. Look for the historical markers that depict highlights of the battle. Admission is free to the park and the San Jacinto Museum of History, and all facilities are open year round.

San Jacinto Monument & San Jacinto Museum of History

Museum is located inside the San Jacinto Monument

Museum Ph: 281-479-2421
Monument Ph: 281-479-2019
Fee: Admission is free
Fee to the Observation Floor: Adults $3, 11 and under $2
Hours: Open seven days a week (Closed December 24, 25)
       9 a.m. – 6 p.m.

Texas Forever!! The Battle of San Jacinto is featured in the Jesse H. Jones Theater for Texas Studies in the Monument. Shown every hour from 10 a.m. – 5 p.m. (lasts 35 minutes). Nominal admission charge.

As you drive toward the Battleground Complex, you can't miss this towering monument built 100 years after the battle of San Jacinto. The monument dominates the landscape. Ride the elevator to the 489-foot observation floor and enjoy a spectacular panoramic view of the Houston skyline.

The monument is 570 feet high and built of reinforced concrete with Texas fossilized buff limestone on the face. Four bronze doors depict the flags of the six governments that have ruled Texas. There are eight huge panels that contain an engraved brief account of the history of the Texas revolution against Mexico. Here are a few facts:

- The monument shaft is 47 feet square and tapers to 30 feet square at the top where the observation tower is located.
- The star, 35 feet high, is at the apex and weighs 220 tons.
- The total approximate weight of the monument is 70,300,000 pounds.

Be sure to go inside the building and see the museum's exhibits that interpret four centuries of Texas and regional history. The collection has over 100,000 items and 250,000 documents, manuscripts, books, and graphic materials. There is a terrific selection of books for adults and children.

Don't miss seeing the award-winning, multi-image presentation *Texas Forever!! The Battle of San Jacinto*. For thirty-five minutes you'll watch the story of the Texas struggle for freedom come to life, all with 42 projectors, over 3,000 slides, and using the latest computer technology.

Battleship Texas State Historical Park

3527 Battleground Road, La Porte, Texas 77571

Ph: 281-479-2411
Web site: www.tpwd.state.tx.us
Fees: Call 281-479-2431 for information on tours and
    contributions
Hours: Open 7 days a week   10 a.m. – 5 p.m.
        Closed December 24 and 25
        Call for tour information; nominal admission fee

Once recognized as the most powerful warship afloat, the Battleship *Texas* was commissioned in 1914. She was armed with 14-inch guns and powered by two steam-driven, four-cylinder engines. In commissioned service for 32 years, the battleship remained at the forefront of technical advancements in engineering, communications, armor, fire control, and armament. Prior to the introduction of the aircraft carrier, the *Texas* played a powerful role in naval aviation, too.

Battleship USS *Texas* (BB35).
Photo courtesy of Texas Parks and Wildlife , San Jacinto State Historical Park.

This great warship participated in the Allied invasion of North Africa on D-Day and then at Normandy, Iwo Jima, and Okinawa during World War II. The Navy presented the Battleship *Texas* to the people of Texas in 1948, making her the first memorial ship. Since 1988 she has been undergoing a major overhaul in dry dock as part of a long-term restoration. Moored at the battleground, she remains open to the public and welcomes all visitors.

Anahuac National Wildlife Refuge

Anahuac, the Alligator Capital of Texas!
P.O. Box 278, Anahuac, Texas 77514

Ph: 409-267-3337

Outdoor Education Program – free to all schools and organizations – contact the Outdoor Recreation Planner.

For grades K-5, classes are taught by Refuge volunteers & staff.

Reservations required; call as far in advance as possible.

Class length averages 1½ hours and is usually held weekday mornings

Class size is up to 60 students with groups broken out consisting of 10 students and 1 Refuge volunteer leader.

Recent outdoor education at the wildlife refuge has included:

- *Nature Discover*—For kindergartners, lasting one hour, this class encourages awareness and appreciation of nature. Students use their five senses as they explore the wildlife refuge world.

- *Nature's Internet*—For grade 1, lasting one hour, this class is full of lively hands-on activities that teach students all about food chains and habitat.

- *Amazing Adaptations*—For grade 2, lasting 1½ hours, the students become nature scientists and learn to compare and analyze adaptation characteristics that reward particular plants and animals with special advantages. Students also look at how different birds adapt in relation to their ecosystems.

- *Insect Exploration*—For grade 3, lasting 1½ hours, this class is highly interactive. After a brief discussion of insects and metamorphosis, the students take on the guise of nature detectives, grab their nets and search for insects to collect, then examine their live specimens.

- *W.O.W. (Wonders of Wetlands)*—For grade 4, lasting 1½ hours, students gain a better understanding of the types, benefits, uses, and future of wetlands. Using their aquatic nets, the participants gather and identify many inhabitants of the refuge's freshwater and saltwater marshes.

- *Reptile Mania*—For grade 5, lasting 1½ hours, students examine ectothermia (cold-bloodedness) and cast their eye toward alligators, snakes, turtles, and other amphibians. The students will take a look at preserved and biocast molded specimens, and if they're lucky, they'll see live alligators.

Anahuac "Gators." © Elaine L. Galit, 2000.

All classes are located outdoors on Anahuac's National Wildlife Refuge, and students learn about the natural world through hands-on educational activities.

Other Listings

Bayou Wildlife Park

5050 FM 517, Alvin, Texas 77511
(Route 6, Box 808)

Ph: 281-337-6376
Fees: Call to verify fees
      Adults – $8.95   Children (3-12) – $5.50
      One child under 3 free with adult
Hours: Call to verify hours during summer months
      Tues. – Fri.   10 a.m. – 3 p.m.
      Sat., Sun.   10 a.m. – 4 p.m.
      September – February: Closed Mondays
(Park is subject to closing during inclement weather.)

Many people are concerned about the threat to a number of Earth's animals and birds. They're becoming endangered, some even extinct, because of poachers, chemicals, and the removal of natural habitat. This park is a good place to introduce children to the work naturalists do every day. Here's a start. Grab your kids and your camera and explore this private 86 acres of natural habitat. What better way to study the animals while learning how to protect them.

You can tour the prairie and woods on a tram while a guide delivers an exciting and interesting talk, stopping along the way to allow you to feed the animals.

This is a great educational adventure, especially for pre-K and kindergarten classes. They will learn the importance of taking care of wild animals. While exploring the farm animal petting area, children can observe how mother goats feed their babies.

This outstanding park is home to 40 species of animals and birds.

Tips:

- While no food is available, there are picnic areas.
- Great for birthday parties, churches, schools, day care centers, and scouts.
- No pets or alcoholic beverages are allowed.
- No cooking in the park.
- Periodically, new animals are introduced into the park. Ask about the nonprofit *Endangered Species Program*. They are trying to obtain additional endangered species to encourage reproduction and breeding.
- The tram ride runs about every 20 minutes and lasts approximately 40 minutes.
- Strollers are not needed outside of the main barnyard.
- Buckets of animal food may be purchased at the entrance for $2.
- Remember to take sunscreen and insect repellent.

Dolphin Watch

Pier 22 at Harborside Dr., Galveston, Texas

Ph: 409-765-1700

E-mail: harbortour@aol.com

Fees: Adults and Seniors $12   Children $10
Confirm prices

Hours: Hours vary due to weather. They can be 8:30 a.m. or 10:30 a.m., depending on time of year and weather. It is recommended that you call. Reservations required.

Note: Most of the Galveston sites have a map at their web site.

Board the *Seagull II* for dolphin watching in Galveston's historic harbor and enjoy an excursion dedicated solely to observing dolphins at play. Learn about the dolphins' habitat and characteristics, and see them up-close and personal.

The ferries in Galveston are also great for dolphin watching.
Photo courtesy of the Galveston Convention and Visitors Bureau.

Fort St. Louis Archeological Project

Texas Historical Commission (THC)
113 West Santa Rosa, P.O. Box 2207 Victoria, TX 77902-2207

Ph: 361-570-1356
Fax: 361-570-8092
E-mail: fslap@tisd.net
Web site: wwwthc.state.tx.us

Fort St. Louis is a great place to take your budding archeologist or history buff. Established by French colonists under La Salle in 1685 and occupied until 1688, Fort St. Louis was the first attempt by Europeans to colonize Texas. Later, in 1722, the Spanish came in search of the French colony, which had already been destroyed, and established the first presidio in Texas at this site.

The Texas Historical Commission (THC) is now conducting the Fort St. Louis Archeological Project. As part of the project, the THC has initiated the Fort St. Louis Public Education Program to educate teachers, students, and the general public about project goals, ongoing investigation results, and preservation. Highlights of the program include:

- A web site allowing viewers to experience the Fort St. Louis archeological investigations through updated video clips.

- Scheduled visits to the THC Fort St. Louis Project Public Archeology Laboratory in the historic Ryan building in the heart of downtown Victoria, Texas. Visitors can tour Fort St. Louis and *La Bette* shipwreck exhibits that tell the story of La Salle and his colony in Texas. Youngsters also will enjoy the working lab where newly discovered artifacts are processed daily.

- Scheduled slide presentations and hands-on artifact demon-strations are available for showing at your school or educational facility.

For scheduling lab visits, school programs, and further informa-tion, please contact: Maureen Brown, Fort St. Louis Project Education Coordinator at 361-570-1356 or e-mail: maureenb @tisd.net.

NOAA/NMFS Sea Turtle Facility

NOAA National Marine Fisheries Service
Southeast Fisheries Science Center Galveston Laboratory
4700 Avenue U, Galveston, Texas 77551

Ph: 409-766-3670
NMFS official web site: http://galveston.ssp.nmfs.gov/galv/
Hours: Tours Tuesday, Thursday and Saturday
      10:00 a.m., 11:00 a.m., 1:00 p.m., 2:00 p.m.
      Closed Sunday
Groups: Groups of less than 8 are welcome without reservation at
    scheduled tour times. Groups of 8+ must call and schedule a
    tour.
Fee: Tours are free
Parking: Free

Note: No food or drink allowed; handicap accessible restrooms and drinking fountain available on site.

Tip: Sea turtles are in the facility year round. Best time to see the hatchlings is August through November. Best time to see larger turtles is December through May.

You need to remember this facility is not a public aquarium or zoo. Instead, it is a government research facility "dedicated to raising threatened and endangered sea turtles in captivity." This is an international effort and part of a cooperative conservation program with Mexico and Florida. The lab also functions as a hospital for the sea turtles.

Before you visit, go to the web sites provided where you'll find a virtual tour of the facility. Others have plenty of photographs and give you a good idea of what is in store when you do visit. There are 600 live sea turtles living in 30 saltwater tanks, with no fence or glass covering them to get between you and the turtles. Children have the opportunity to get very close; the lab only asks that you *do not touch*. Tour guides will handle the turtles and show

Turtles. Photo courtesy of NMFS SEFC Galveston Lab.

them to you. This visit is full of live exhibits, plenty of Kemp's ridley and loggerhead sea turtles, even turtle skulls and shells that can be touched. Tours last 30-60 minutes and are age appropriate. This is a tremendous learning opportunity for adults as well as children.

Seawolf Park

Pelican Island via Seawolf Parkway (51st St.),
Galveston, Texas

Ph: 409-744-5738
Go to the web site for a virtual tour of Galveston Island at:
http://www.utmb.edu/galveston/attractions/seawolf.html

Fees: *Fishing*   Adults $3   Kids $2
        Submarine   Adults $4   Kids $2
        Parking $5, and Busses $10

Hours: Open dawn to dusk. Check hours before you go.

> **Tip:** *Strollers are not recommended due to narrow passages and stairs aboard the submarine.*

Pelican Island is the small island to the north of Galveston that is separated from the main island by the Galveston Ship Channel. Now dedicated to the memory of Navy men lost at sea during World War II, the park is named after the *Seawolf* submarine lost in WWII and was opened in 1974. The park displays the WWII submarine *Cavalla* and the destroyer escort *Stewart* as well as other military vehicles.

Enjoy the pavilion with its perfect view of passing international freighters and tankers and a fishing pier. Off the pier, at the entrance to the Galveston Ship Channel, is the wreckage of the 421-foot concrete tanker ship the *Selma*, one of 12 experimental concrete ships. Its maiden voyage to Tampico ended when it hit a jetty. The *Selma* was returned to Galveston in 1923 where she now rests. Since then, the *Selma* has unknowingly been part of a second experiment as an artificial reef.

Seawolf Park rock fishing.
Photo courtesy of the Galveston Convention and Visitors Center.

Winnie, Texas – Agricultural Historical Museum (AHM)

Winnie Area Chamber of Commerce, P.O. Box 147
Winnie, Texas 77665

Ph: 409-296-2231
Hours: The AHM is open for tours by appointment. Please call
   409-296-2231.

Winnie, Texas, is an oasis between the metropolitan areas of Houston, Galveston, and Beaumont/Port Arthur. This town of roughly 5,000 is known for its neighborly atmosphere and central location. Drive beyond the towering skyscenes of Houston or past the refinery specked horizon of the Golden Triangle and enter this land of rice fields and cattle.

   The Agricultural Historical Museum is a tribute to the history of the farmers and ranchers who have been the backbone of this community. Located behind the Texas Rice Festival/Chamber of Commerce offices on LeBlanc Street, the museum houses authentic antique tractors, farming equipment, photos, and the airplane that planted the first aerially seeded rice crop in Texas. In addition, the Winnie Santa Fe Depot, which was established in 1905, has been relocated alongside the Agricultural Historical Museum and will soon be restored. This museum will house many other items relating to the overall history of the area.

 **Toolbox Tips**

All About Alligators

- Anahuac is the Alligator Capital of Texas. For information on the Texas GATORFEST held every September and on alligators in the Anahuac area contact:

  The Anahuac Area Chamber of Commerce
  P.O. Box R, Anahuac, Texas 77514
  Ph: 409-267-4190
  Web site: www.texasgatorfest.com

- The American alligator is a member of the crocodile family, whose members are living fossils from the Age of Reptiles, having survived on earth for 200 million years. Brazos Bend State Park and the Anahuac National Wildlife Refuge are two great places for "meeting up" with alligators in the Houston area.

- Once considered an endangered species, the American alligator was pronounced fully recovered in 1987, making it one of the first endangered species success stories.

- Before taking a visit to see alligators, help your child learn about them. Kids are fascinated by alligators, and there are many books and web sites devoted to the subject. Alligators are diggers and create "gator holes." An alligator uses its mouth and claws to clear out the space, shoves its body in, and, slashing its powerful tail, wallows out a depression that stays full of water in the wet season and holds water after the rains stop. They often create hidden dens by tunneling as far as 20 feet and enlarging the end to make a chamber. Why is this so important to the marsh and the other animals in it?

Aquariums

- Take a trip to a pet store that specializes in aquariums. Find out what it would take to set up a small ten-gallon aquarium. What kind of fish would you want to put in the tank? Read up on the fish and how to take care of them. What do you have to know to keep a tank operating? Decide if you really want to have one. If not, make a drawing of your perfect aquarium and the chosen fish.

- Visit other aquariums such as the Moody Garden Aquarium Pyramid. Go on the Internet and locate other aquariums. Did you know there are plans for a major public aquarium to be built in Austin, Texas?

Pirates — Jean Lafitte

- Jean Lafitte is a mysterious character whose story is full of contradictions. Was he a pirate or a patriot? Did he really smuggle or was he conducting business? Some called him a hero and a legend, others a murderer and a thief. Find out more about him before going to Galveston.

- Buried treasure is a lure to many, and Jean Lafitte's reported treasure buried on Galveston Island has eluded everyone for years. How do people today look for buried treasure? Where would you look?

- Read *Treasure Island*, a famous pirate story by Robert Louis Stevenson. There are also several video versions. Try the Treasure Island web site.

- Pirates were the marauders of the high seas for years and often did their deeds under the cover of kings. What place in history do they have? How did they help the kings? Read about some of the infamous pirates and draw some pictures illustrating their stories.

The Great Storm — Galveston, Texas, September 8, 1900

- To this day, the Great Storm of 1900 is still the nation's deadliest storm with the loss of at least six thousand people. Before going to Galveston, go to the Rosenberg Library web site to discover more about the storm. They have massive records.

- Read *Isaac's Storm* for an absolutely stunning recount of the 1900 storm. This is a book for adults but is well written, and teens should be able to read the story. The author's web site, www.isaacsstorm.com, has great links for more information.

- Weather is a fascinating subject. Encourage your child to learn more about the various types of weather, particularly hurricanes, as they are common to the Houston area. Some scientists keep a daily weather log. The Museum of Natural Science downtown has an excellent exhibit on weather and features KHOU-TV's Dr. Neil Frank. Also check out KHOU's web site at www.khou.com.

- Help your child track hurricanes during the next hurricane season. Many local retailers and local television stations come together to produce excellent tracking maps that are readily and easily available. Watch the Weather Channel.

Texas History — Reenactors

- Reenactors are people who have an interest in history, its study and preservation, and re-create history with astonishing historical accuracy in their dress, manners, and knowledge. It is common for reenactors to be featured in movies such as *Gettysburg the Founding Fathers*. There are local reenactors who re-create Texas history. A local Civil War Reenactor group is open to everyone. Find out when they will be re-creating the next event or if there is one planned for the Battle of San Jacinto. Their web site has many related links. Contact information is:

Houston Civil War Roundtable
P.O. Box 4215
Houston, Texas 77210-4215
Web site: www.houstcwrt.com
E-mail: Houstcwrt@aol.com

 # Resources

Books, Brochures, and Magazine Information

Across the Big Blue Sea: An Ocean Wildlife Book—"An extraordinary ocean wildlife book for beginners..."—*Kirkus Reviews*

Isaac's Storm: A Man, a Time, and the Deadliest Hurricane in History by Erik Larson—"A gripping account...fascinating to its core, and all the more compelling for being true."—*The New York Times Book Review*

That Terrible Texas Weather by Johnny D. Boggs. True-life stories of survival in natural catastrophes including the Great Storm of 1900.

About Reptiles: A Guide for Children by Cathryn Sill. Recommended for ages 3-8. Depicts how physical characteristics, habitat, movement, feeding and hunting behavior, and life cycle can vary in different kinds of reptiles, including the American alligator.

Crocodiles and Alligators by Cloudsley-Thompson, J.L. Biology, behavior, and contact with humans discussed.

Related Organizations

Rosenberg Library, Galveston, Texas
Ph: 409-763-8854
Web site: www.rosenberg.com

Located at 23rd and Sealy in Galveston. The library opened in 1904 and is recognized as Texas's first public library.

Related Web Sites

www.galveston.ssp.nmfs.gov/galv/seaturtles.htm
   Great site for the kids with a 32-page coloring book and educational activity book to download

www.galveston.ssp.nmfs.gov/galv/seaturtles.htm
   Very kid-friendly page

http://galveston.ssp.nmfs.gov/galv/turtles/brochure/barn.htm
   Virtual tour of facility and MAP! All can be downloaded.

Princess America
   http://www.princessamerica.org/december97/barn.html
   A look inside the sea turtle barn

Alligators

Wildlife of the Alligator River
www.carolina.com

Bayou Pierre Alligator Farm
   http://www.cp-tel.net/bpap/alligat.html
   Natchitoches, Louisiana—Come explore the unique, mysterious, and exciting world of the American alligator in Louisiana.

Snakes-n-Scales and Turtle Tales
www.snakes-n-scales.com
   This site offers environmental education programs for all ages with an emphasis on learning through enjoyment. Great links and programs, too, such as *Fossils, a Walk Through Time*, and *The Good, the Icky, and the Slimy.*

Aquariums

www.tennis.org
   The Tennessee Aquarium, located in Chattanooga, is the world's largest freshwater aquarium. Experience the aquarium

online, learn about freshwater ecosystems, fish, jellyfish, crustaceans, mussels, amphibians, reptiles and more. This site is a wonderful resource for parents, students, and teachers. Visit amazing animals, check out the IMAX theater, and even plan your visit to the aquarium, all from the convenience of your own PC.

National Aquarium

www.aqua.net

Baltimore's Inner Harbor, where you'll find fun information about animals, exhibits, conservation efforts, and the institution itself. Enjoy interactive games and even a learning page for students and teachers.

National Museum of Natural History

www.nmnh.org

This site illustrates a great diversity of fish, generally relying on the vast resources of the national fish collection. The fish collection, at the National Museum of Natural History, is the largest in the world, with approximately 500,000 lots (a lot consists of all specimens of a species from the same time and place) and about 8 million specimens.

SeaWorld

www.seaworld.org

The online version of Bush Garden's SeaWorld adventure park. Great links to educational resources, educational programs, animal resources and much more. Learn more about Shamu TV adventure camps and see the live penguin cam!

Waikiki Aquarium

www.otted.hawaii.edu/aquarium/

Take a virtual tour of the Waikiki Aquarium, founded in 1904, the third oldest public aquarium in the United States. The exhibits, programs, and research focus on the aquatic life of Hawaii and the tropical Pacific. Endangered and threatened species are among the unique organisms that visitors can see and appreciate.

Aquarium of the Americas
> http://www.auduboninstitute.org/html/aa_aquariumain.html
> From the Audubon Institute site—great site with many things to see.

Reefkeepers.com
> An on-line aquarium superstore that is designed to meet all of your aquarium needs. Whether you are a beginner or an expert, they have the fish, inverts, and equipment that you need.

Pirates

National Geographic Kids—Pirates
> http://www.nationalgeographic.com/features/97/pirates/mania.html
> Don't miss this site!

A Pirate's Life
> http://www.themeunits.com/Pirates.html
> A treasure chest of pirate facts and activities for grades K-3

The "Scoop" Adventure Page
> http://www.friend.ly.net/scoop/adventure/index.html
> Interactive pirate stories for young readers

Treasure Island Unit
> http://www.dreamcatchers.net/treasure/introduction.html
> An outstanding site for teachers, kids, and adults. Study piracy while you read *Treasure Island*. Great projects.

Pirate Pete's Treasure Ship
> www.piratepete.com
> Many activities and fun for children. Print out pirate color sheets, activity booklet and more.

Pirates of the Spanish Main
> http://www.sonic.net/~press

A great site and wonderful graphics. Plenty of information on pirates in general. Great source to find out more about those really famous pirates. Even has a Tall Ship Adventure link.

Weather and Storms

Dr. Neil Frank's Weather Page
www.khou.com
Has a great Hurricane Central

National Oceanic and Atmospheric Administration (NOAA)
www.noaa.com
An organization of the Department of Commerce, NOAA is composed of the National Ocean Service, National Weather Service, National Marine Fisheries Service, National Environmental Satellite Data, and Information Service, and Office of Oceanic and Atmospheric Research.

National Hurricane Center
www.nhc.com
NHC maintains a continuous watch on tropical cyclones over the Atlantic, Caribbean, Gulf of Mexico, and the Eastern Pacific from May 15 through November 30.

FEMA/Tropical Storm and Hurricane Watch Information
www.fema.com
This site from The Federal Emergency Management Agency contains the latest information on storms as well as a guide to hurricane preparedness that can be downloaded.

Weather.com
www.weather.com
The official site of the Weather Channel

www.1900storm.com
This site is a service of the *Galveston County Daily News* in conjunction with the Galveston 1900 Storm Commemoration Committee.

Galveston Island

www.galvestonhistoricalfoundation.com
Includes a list of local attractions and a calendar of events

Galveston, Texas Travel & Visitor Guide
www.galveston.com
Offering hotels, restaurants, events, attractions, arts, entertainment, museums, and real estate

History

www.reenactorspage.com
Online "magazine" devoted to reenacting and the Civil War

6

Magic Carpet Ride!

"I tell parents and grandparents all the time to take them [children] to the historical sites. There are thousands and thousands of sites. Take them there. You'd be amazed at how it can catch them up. Sit at the campsite in the evening, bring out the old journals written by the people who were there, and read to them out loud, 'At this site...' I promise you..."
 —Stephen Ambrose, author and historian

Children are curious by nature; they are the eternal questioners, but often they view history as something that happened to a bunch of people who died a long time ago. As adults, our task is to stimulate their imagination and encourage their exploration of the world. How do we make history and geography interesting and alive to kids? The best way is through a story, by making it "up front and personal." Tell them a good story, take them places where they can experience the time, the period, the people. As Arthur Schlesinger said, "Nothing is more fun or more fascinating than the consideration of how people lived in the past."

History is a grand adventure. Stories about the past abound. In their imaginations children are transported. Geography, with its emphasis on place, transforms into a magic carpet that carries children away to relive early civilizations and discover lost worlds. The combination of both leads to questions of how place affects people and, in turn, how do people shape place?

The benefits of studying history and geography are vast. Children have the opportunity to learn from the experience of past generations and receive a guide to the present and the future. The impact of place on people becomes evident. One of the best local examples is the effect of the great hurricane on Galveston Island more than one hundred years ago. The island is now fifteen feet higher than it was prior to the storm. In four minutes the floodwaters rose fifteen feet, covering the island and the mainland for miles. The water reached Fort Bend County, more than fifty miles away. Prior to the storm, the island had been prosperous and proud, vying for national status with its port. After the storm and the death of an estimated six thousand people, Houston became one of the busiest ports and Galveston never recovered.

There are a number of other ways to bring history to life. Encourage children to read historical fiction. Often the novelist can reveal more than historians can. They can tell more and re-create a feel for the past. The History Channel brings history to a large audience in a highly visual way.

Documentaries are useful, even fiction films, but remember they do not present a literal truth. Visiting historical sites such as San Jacinto Battleground Park allows children to touch the past.

When asked about the value of a living history facility, Nancy Porter, George Ranch's Director of Marketing said, "Learning about Texas history is great but experiencing it is a whole different story... It's feeling, touching, it's smelling life in early Texas." An area's industry and economics has a historical influence on the area and the people. Local children can meet history face-to-face by visiting:

- *George Ranch*—A time capsule where early Texas living history programs are staged.

- *The Forbidden Gardens*—A miniature replica of the Forbidden City of China's Middle Kingdom.

- *Holocaust Museum Houston*—A tremendous place that teaches children the consequences of hatred, bigotry, and apathy and provides children today a place to meet those who survived the persecution.

- *Fort Bend Museum*—A great place to touch local history and learn how previous Texans dealt with World War II events.

- *Alabama-Coushatta Reservation*—An opportunity to experience another culture.

Houston is rich in history. Even today during our daily lives, we create and encounter live history. During the past several years, we've experienced the death of Princess Diana and Mother Theresa, and the historical 2000 election still impacts our daily lives. What follows are a number of places in Houston that practice great storytelling.

George Ranch Historical Park

Rounding Up Texas History!
10215 FM 762, P.O. Box 1248, Richmond, Texas 77406

Ph: 281-545-9212 or 281-343-0218
Fax: 281-343-9316
Web site: www.georgeranch.org
Fees: Adults $7.50   Seniors 55+ $6.50
          Children 3-12 $4
Hours: Open daily 9 a.m. – 5 p.m.
          Closed January 1, Thanksgiving, December 24, 25, 31
          School and group tours offered daily by reservation only.
          Group, special programs, and special annual events

> *Note:* The George Ranch Historical Park is a living history project of the Fort Bend Museum Association and the George Foundation.

Time travel is possible. The George Ranch is a 480-acre living history park. The park is at the center of a 23,000-acre working cattle ranch and provides time travel to the 1830s, the 1890s, and the 1930s. Experience life with one family through four generations. Your child will brush up close against Texas history.

- Reenactors portray Henry and Nancy Jones, two of Stephen F. Austin's first Texas colonists. See and touch a pioneer dogtrot cabin and barn. Life in the 1830s included daily chores of corn grinding, dutch oven cooking, spinning cotton, woodworking, and tending livestock. You'll have hands-on activities as you work with the Joneses.

Kids plowing at 1830s ranch. Photo courtesy George Ranch Historical Park.

- Next is the Victorian mansion of J.H.P. Davis and his wife, Belle. Step into a full Victorian life. The mansion is complete with outbuildings including servants quarters, carriage house, greenhouse, and grape arbor. Nearby is the local blacksmith's shop where the blacksmith demonstrates how to work iron and use period tools. Wander over to the cowboy camp and chuck wagon and get steeped in cowboy folklore. Hands-on activities include roping, mock branding, and campfire cooking.

- The next generation of this family endured the Great Depression of the 1930s. Mamie and A.P. George's ranch now had the cistern house, cookhouse, and the smokehouse. Cowboys rode, roped, and worked cattle around the original dipping vat, pens, tack barn, and horse barn. Black cowboys also worked the ranch, and their contributions are shown. The final treat is the big treehouse built in the 1930s.

Davis house and black cowboy. Photo courtesy George Ranch Historical Park.

Reenactors and car at 1930s house. Photo courtesy George Ranch Historical Park.

Education Programs

For detailed information on student programs, call or e-mail the Education Department at education@georgeranch.org.

- *Self-Guided Tour*—Students visit the various time periods conducted by costumed interpreters who help the students move through 150 years of Texas history. They witness history in action as costumed characters re-enact daily chores and activities such as weaving and spinning, blacksmith forging, and many cowboy activities. This tour is suitable for all ages. One adult (admitted free) required for every 12 students. Extra chaperones are charged. A deposit will be required. Ages range from 3 yrs. to 8th grade ($4), 9th grade to 12th ($6.50), and adults ($7). Prices are per person.

- *Self-Guided Tour & Hands-On Activity*—All four programs include self-guided tour plus the activity in the cost.

- *Gone to Texas*—A challenging program that offers a unique role-playing activity for older students. Students become Texas colonists, part of the Texas settlement movement. For 25-65 students 6th – 12th grade, the time length is 60-90 minutes.

- *Pioneer*—For younger students. As participants, they discuss the toys and games played in the pioneer days, and make a corn husk doll and a simple dart game. For 25 or less, 1st – 5th grade students, the program lasts 50 minutes.

- *Victorian*—Students enter an 1890s chuck wagon camp and participate in all the steps of preparing chuck wagon fare. For 25 or less, 1st – 5th grade students, the program lasts 50 minutes.

- *Ranching*—These lucky 1st – 5th graders gather around the cowboy's supply wagon and join in all the activities. They may draw, tell a story, write a cowboy poem, or design a brand. For 25 students or less, the program lasts 50 minutes.

In addition to these learning opportunities, the George Ranch also conducts interesting and enjoyable summer programs that are open to the public.

forbidden Gardens

Discover the Mysteries of Imperial China!
23500 Franz Road, Katy, Texas 77493

Ph: 281-347-8000
Web site: www.forbidden-gardens.com
Fees: Adults $10   Children age 6-8 $5
         Seniors 60+ & Students with college ID $5
         Groups of 25+ people $5 per person
         Children 5 and under are admitted free with a paid
         admission
Free Parking
Hours: Wed. – Sun.   10 a.m. – 5 p.m.
          Open until 7 p.m. during summer months.
          Closed Monday and Tuesday for prearranged tours.

Beverages are available. Souvenirs and film sold at the Central Court gift shop. Wheelchairs and strollers available.

> "In 15th century China, the color red symbolized good luck and the brides wore red dresses and rode in red vehicles to give them good fortune in their marriages."
> —from Forbidden Gardens brochure

Here's a further opportunity to become immersed in another culture, this time 15th-century China during the Ming Dynasty. Artifacts, exhibits, and more reveal China's Middle Kingdom and its mysterious past. Replicated here is one of the most remarkable archeology finds of the century, the more than 7,000 life-size terra-cotta soldiers and horses guarding the Emperor Qin's tomb.

Forbidden Gardens is a city in miniature and replicates not only the First Emperor's terra-cotta army, but also the Calming of the Heart Lodge, a favorite of the emperors and empresses of the Ming Dynasty for vacation or rest, and the canal city of Suzhou. The vaults containing the terra-cotta soldiers also brought forth a vast armory of metal weapons buried for over two thousand years. An exhibit of the city of Suzhou depicts typical lifestyles of the residents of both the outer rural areas and the wealthy inner city. The likeness of nine dragons, a dragon being a symbol of the emperor, are woven into the mighty throne and reveal the extravagance of this empire. The empress' red sedan chair is equally as ornate.

Forbidden City exhibit. Photo courtesy of Forbidden Gardens.

Holocaust Museum Houston
Education Center and Memorial

5401 Caroline Street, Houston, Texas

Ph: 713-942-8000
Fax: 713-942-7953
Web site: www.hmh.org
Fee: No admission fee
Hours: Mon. – Fri. 9 a.m. – 5 p.m.
  Sat. – Sun. 12 noon – 5 p.m.
Tours: Guided tours are available for all visitors on Saturday and Sunday. Weekend tours run at 12:30 p.m., 1:30 p.m., 2:30 p.m., and 3:30 p.m. Docent-led tours can be scheduled for schools and groups of 10 or more. Tours are available in Spanish, English, and French. To arrange a docent-led tour, please call Visitor Services at 713-942-8000, ext. 102 or contact us at tours@hmh.org.

"The Holocaust Museum is a living testimonial to the millions who perished in the Holocaust, a place to honor our friends and neighbors who survived and a source of education for this and future generations."

The story of the horrors of the Holocaust is told at Holocaust Museum Houstn by focusing on the lives and experiences of local people who lived through it. A state sponsored persecution and annihilation of European Jewry by the Nazis and their collaborators occurred between 1933 and 1945, the end of World War II.

- *Voices*—A film featuring testimonies by local Holocaust survivors plays continuously.
- *Between Darkness and Light*—A collection of paintings that depict the rescue of Jews by Danes and Bulgarians.

- *Rescuers*—A new exhibit of photographs by Gay Block and Malka Drucker spotlights people who rescued victims from Nazi persecution.

The education center explores issues of the Holocaust, racism, and the consequences of hate. The museum is the first institution of its kind in the Southwest. Each month an average of 6,000 people visit the museum.

Camp section of the Permanent Exhibit at the Holocaust Museum Houston.
Photo courtesy of Holocaust Museum Houston.

Bearing Witness: A Community Remembers

The core of the museum is the permanent exhibit, which is unique in its emphasis on Houston area Holocaust survivors. The museum tells the story of the origin of Judaism and life before World War II, to the rise of the Nazi Party, the Holocaust, and through the aftermath of the "Final Solution."

- *Josef and Edith Mincberg Gallery*—The Mincberg Gallery hosts artistic exhibits of paintings, drawings, photography, and artifacts on specific Holocaust related subjects that give the viewer an artist's perspective.

- *The Lack Family Memorial Room*—The award-winning Memorial Room provides visitors with a quiet place for reflection on the lessons learned from the Holocaust, gathered from the permanent and art exhibitions. The Memorial Room contains *The Wall of Remembrance*, *The Wall of Tears*, *The Wall of Hope*, and *The Memorial Wall*.

- *Eric Alexander Garden of Hope*—The garden memorializes the 1.5 million children who perished in the Holocaust, as well as honors the eternal spirit of all children.

- *Boniuk Library and Resource Center*—More than 4,000 books on the history of the Jews, the Holocaust, post Holocaust, and related subjects are kept in the library. In addition to books, the library lends videos and posters. Don't miss the *Original Stories Project*, which contains over 200 oral testimonies of Holocaust survivors, liberators, and witnesses.

> **Note:** For more information on the contents of the library, please call Ginny Harrell, Librarian and Director of Archives and Research Services at 713-942-8000, ext. 110.

Education Programs

The museum provides educational services for public school districts, private middle and high schools, home schools, universities, colleges, and libraries. The Speakers Bureau has provided Holocaust survivors, and they have touched the hearts and minds of thousands.

Holocaust Museum Houston's Curriculum Trunk Program

Each trunk contains multimedia tools including videos, posters, CDs, CD-ROMs, artifact kits, maps, classroom sets of books, lessons plans, and student activities. Trunks are shipped nationwide to requesting teachers on a first-come, first-served basis.

"Students gained a broader insight into the prejudice, hatred, and violence that led to one of the greatest tragic events in our world history"—Lesly Christine Stern

An important resource for educators, they have been developed for use by elementary, middle school, high school, and college educators. Not only do they assist in teaching the historical facts relating to the Holocaust, but more importantly, the lessons of prejudice awareness and the consequences of apathy in society. These trunks have been as far away as the U.S. Army bases in Italy, Germany, Japan, and Bosnia.

To sponsor a trunk, contact Alexia Bres at 713-942-8000, ext. 121. To borrow a trunk, contact Catherine Pees 713-942-8000, ext. 120.

Fort Bend Museum

Get Your Hands On Texas!
500 Houston Street, Richmond, Texas 77469

Ph: 281-342-6478
Web site: www.fortbendmuseum.org
Fees: Adults $3   55+ $2.50
         Children 3-12 $2   Children 13+ $3
Hours: Tues. – Fri.   9 a.m. – 5 p.m.
              Sat.   10 a.m. – 5 p.m.
              Sun.   1 p.m. – 5 p.m.
         Closed Thanksgiving, Christmas & New Years Days

The Old West and the South come together in what is often called one of the state's best museums. The early Texan colonists, led by Stephen F. Austin, settled in grant lands between the Brazos and San Bernard Rivers. This museum is a great point to begin exploration of the area's rich heritage. The complex includes a sharecropper's cabin, B. F. Terry and Terry's Texas Rangers exhibits, the Long Smith Cottage, the 1883 John M. Moore Home, and the McFarlane House. Eras depicted are those of the Texas revolution, plantation life, the Civil War, ranching, and the sugar industry. Texan heroine Jane Long owned one of the homes from the 1840s.

Education Programs

The museum offers a number of educational programs. To schedule a school program, call the Education Coordinator at 281-342-6478. Cost is $3 per student and the program can be designed to fit your needs. All programs meet TAAS objectives. Groups booking field trips receive teacher packets to help students prepare for the museum learning experience. Programs last 1½ - 2 hours.

- New for educators—the *Traveling Trunk & Exhibits* are free to teachers.
- *Laws of our Land 1896 – Present*—A lesson in civics, history, and physical fitness are combined in this program as students tour the homes of three important political figures in Richmond and Fort Bend County: Congressman John M. Moore Sr., Judge John M. Moore Jr., and Mayor Hilmar Moore. 6th grade – adult.
- *Victorian Times in Texas 1890 – 1910*—Participants experience life during the Victorian era and will attend a "one room school" and tour the home of John and Lottie Moore. The Moore's children come alive as the students learn games from that era. 3rd grade – adult.
- *Smith Family at Home 1860s*—Students take on the role of the 15-member Smith family and dress in simple costumes. They'll tour the Long-Smith Cottage, learn how historic homes are preserved, and hand-tint a Smith family photograph. 4 yrs. – 3rd grade.

- *Texas: Land of Beginnings 1820s – 1836*—Relive the Runaway Scrape when pioneers and soldiers clashed in the fight for Texas Independence. A tour of the gallery of early Texas history completes the program.

- *Texas for Young'Uns 1890s*—Children explore corn shelling, Victorian dress-up, and toys from the 19th century. 4 yrs. – 3rd grade.

- *Museum Gallery Tour*—Early pioneers uprooted their families and came to Texas. Why? Exhibits and artifacts bring Stephen F. Austin's American colonists alive.

- *Textiles in Texas*—Ever wonder how children's clothes were made two hundred years ago? Find out about ginning, carding, and spinning cotton, weaving fabric, and making quilts.

- *Digging into the Past*—If you respond to the lure of archeology, make sure you participate in a simulated dig and view the many artifacts.

Everyday Life—1840-1890

- *Our Little House*—In the historic Long-Smith Cottage students tour Jane Long's house and gain an elementary understanding of historic preservation. They can compare the differences between early urban homes and houses today.

- *Lottie's Children*—Visit the historic Moore Home and discover how the children of Lottie and Congressman John Moore lived. Students participate in daily chores including washing clothes (when weather permits), drawing water from the well, churning butter, and shelling corn.

- *Old Attic Trunk*—Learn about families at the turn of the century as you step back in time to discover the treasures in an old attic trunk.

Our Patriotic Past

- *Moore Home Tour*—Visit the historic Moore Home and discover the beauty of the 1880s mansion interpreted in the style of the 1940s. The home contains item owned by Congressman John M. Moore and his son, Judge John M. Moore Jr. Hilmar Moore, grandson of Congressman Moore, has been mayor of Richmond since 1949.

- *Victory – The People's Part*—Small home gardens, women working outside the home, children knitting blankets for injured soldiers, recycling, and rationing were part of life for Americans during WWII. Learn how the shortages changed everyday life and resulted in new products.

- *Helping Out*—This program is held on the grounds of the historic Moore Home. Students focus on the work of the American Red Cross and how children helped during WWII. They make and pack bandages for training Red Cross volunteers and discuss how the Red Cross showed they valued the work of the volunteers.

Historic Preservation Programs

- *Richmond Walking Tour*—During this walking tour of historic Richmond, students see historic buildings: the 1896 Richmond Jail, the 1901 Depot, the McFarlane House, and more. This program cannot be booked with any other program—66 students maximum.

- *Our Historic Community*—Students learn community history, explore historic architecture, and discover the contributions of various groups of settlers in Texas. They listen to the story *Community: Past, Present, and Future*.

- *Law & Order in Fort Bend County*—Students tour the museum exhibit at the 1896 Richmond Jail and learn about the early beginnings of the Fort Bend County sheriff's department and the Richmond police force.

- *Collecting, Caring & Sharing*—This program explores how, why, and what people collect, including museums. Learn how to care for collections, how to exhibit them, and how to teach others using your collections.

- *The Morton Cemetery Tour*—An optional replacement program for any other element. One of the oldest cemeteries in the state provides an excellent opportunity to learn about local history.

- *Outreach Programs*—Some programs can be adapted for presentation at your school. Let them know your needs and interest.

Alabama-Coushatta Indian Reservation

Explore the Beauty of Native American Traditions
Alabama-Coushatta Tribe
Rt. 3 Box 640 Livingston, Texas 77351

Ph: 800-444-3507 and 409-563-4391
Web site: www.alabama-coushatta.com
Camping facilities available 800-926-9038
Open Late May to early September – Call for dates
Open weekends March – May and November
Closed December – February
Fees:　Admission is free. Fee for tribal dance and tour.
　　　　Group discounts available for groups of 25 or more.
Hours: Mon. & Tues. – Gift Shop and Museum open only
　　　　Wed. – Sun. – Full Activities
　　　　Mon. – Sat.　10:00 a.m. – 6:00 p.m.
　　　　Sunday　　　12:30 p.m. – 6:00 p.m.

Located 17 miles east of Livingston and 15 miles west of Woodville on U.S. 190.

This 4,593.7-acre reservation is home to the Alabama and Coushatta Indians who are part of southern forest tribes in the Big Thicket. Be transported back into Indian country and the days of the pioneers. See the original styles of Indian homes, campsites, and hunting grounds and hear the sound of drums in the Tribal Dance Square. Colorful Indian dancers perform their cultural dances.

- *Alabama-Coushatta Cultural Center*—Classes in traditional crafts such as pine needle and cane baskets are offered.
- *Annual Powwow*—Held annually during the first weekend in June.
- *Living Indian Village*—Tribal members use traditional skills to make leather items, baskets, and jewelry.
- *Big Thicket tours*—Take a swamp buggy or the miniature railroad to explore the Big Thicket.
- *Recreation*—Take advantage of the camping areas, lake fishing, and swimming.

Toolbox Tips

China and the Forbidden City

1. Take some soft modeling clay and shape your own terra-cotta soldiers and horses.

2. Find a travel book or a *National Geographic* book with stories about China. Cut out images you like and make a collage on China.

3. Go to the library and find books on giant pandas. What do giant pandas do? What do they eat? Where do they live? Draw a picture of giant pandas in their natural habitat.

4. The Chinese zodiac consists of animals such as the dragon and the rat. What animal on the zodiac represents you? What are the animal's traits? Do you have any of those traits?

Cowboys and Western Life

1. Find some recipes for chuck wagon fare and make your own.
2. Go to KG and the Ranger's web site (1999 MWA Harmony Yodeling Champions) and listen to the yodeling, then try it yourself.
3. Get some ordinary rope and practice roping tricks.
4. Attend the Houston Rodeo. Lots of animals, calf scrambles, and chuck wagon races to see.

The Holocaust

Due to the nature of this subject matter, we recommend that parents, leaders, and educators establish a dialogue with the child and be sensitive to the child's emotions and thoughts.

• Read *The Diary of Anne Frank* and other holocaust stories for a real sense of what happened. There is a tremendous amount of information about Anne Frank. Ask your child if he or she could have lived in a small hiding place like Anne did for so many years. What would they have done? Ask him to draw a picture of Anne's hideout.

• Anne Frank kept a diary during her two-year hideout. Have the child keep a journal every day for two weeks. What did your child learn from writing about his or her everyday life? What kinds of things did your child write about?

• Ask your child what can be learned from the terrible ordeal the Jewish people underwent in Germany during World War II. Ask them if they've ever seen or experienced any bigotry.

Resources

Books, Brochures, and Magazine Information

Requiem for a German Past: A Boyhood Among the Nazis by Jurgen Herbst—"Herbst's account of growing up in Nazi Germany from 1928 – 1948 describes a boy's experience of anti-Semitism and militarism from the inside. It is a tale of moral awakening"—Lisa Moellering, Holocaust Museum Houston

The Diary of Anne Frank by Anne Frank—Well-known classic

Schindler's List by Thomas Kenneally—Must read. Steven Spielberg produced an excellent film from this book.

Abe's Story: A Holocaust Memoir by Abram Korn—"Straightforward in its telling and moving in its honesty, this is a poignant reminder of Holocaust atrocities. A worthwhile addition to adult and young collections."—Marcia Welsh, *Library Journal*

Number the Stars by Lois Lowry—A classic book for children

The Devil's Arithmetic by Jane Yolen—Winner of many awards, this book was a Nebula Honor Book.

Cowboy Fun by Monica Hay Cook—Packed full of facts about the lives and times of cowboys in the Old West. Each page includes a hands-on activity for children to do that relates to the historical information.

Abbot's Encyclopedia of Rope Tricks for the Magician compiled by Stewart James—Abbott's classic book on rope magic gives you all the basic moves and manipulations, plus advanced rope work. Dozens of great routines with ordinary rope! For ages 10 to adult; skill level, easy.

Self-working Rope Tricks by Karl Fulves—Learn to do amazing rope tricks instantly, with ordinary rope! Author Karl Fulves has collected 70 foolproof rope tricks that "work themselves." No special skills or sleight-of-hand necessary. A great introduction to rope magic for all ages!

Growing up in Ancient China by Ken Teague

The Legend of Mulan—a Heroine of Ancient China by A. Jiang, Wei; Jiang, Cheng

Related Organizations

Anne Frank Foundation, Prinsengracht 263, NL-1016 GV Amsterdam, The Netherlands.

Related Web Sites

Cowboy Heritage, History, and Heros

www.cow-boy.com

Online reference developed by the Cowboy Heritage Club featuring cowboy life, lore, legend, and more

Buffalo Bill's Wild West

www.buffalobill.com

America's Family Show—Learn about Buffalo Bill's Wild West Show and "Cowboy Cuisine," favorite recipes from over 200 cowboy contributors from the U.S., 19 foreign countries, and Texas.

Gene Autry Oklahoma Museum

http://autry-museum.org/

In the only town named for a movie cowboy, this museum, dedicated to "the singing cowboy" (all of them), has an outstanding collection of memorabilia.

Roy Rogers-Dale Evans web site

www.royrogers.com

Another outstanding site. This one features the late King of the Cowboys and Queen of the West, and their museum in Victorville, California. Parents and teachers: Download the education packet for great activities for kids. (Before the download begins, you are able to review the packet material.)

KG and The Ranger Cowboy and Yodeling
    www.kgandtheranger.com
    1999 WMA Harmony Yodeling Champions—Classic cowboy
    and cowgirl music, cowboy songs from the movie cowboys Roy
    Rogers, Gene Autry, and Patsy Montana, harmony yodeling,
    rope tricks. Old-time country music performances with an
    exciting new feel, with cowboy wisdom, humor, cowboy his-
    tory, and trick rope spinning

www.surfnetkids.com/china.htm
    The best China sites on the web for families (from the *Los
    Angeles Times* Syndicate), rated and reviewed

http://www.intel.com/apac/eng/virtualcity/real.htm
    A virtual tour of the former Imperial Palace including 3D
    modeling from Intel

http://www.beijingtrip.com/attractions/forbidden/index.htm
    Provides a virtual tour of the Imperial Palace Museum from
    Beijing trip. Map and illustrated description of each of the
    main buildings are interwoven with history and anecdotes
    about the imperial family (www.beijingtrip.com has informa-
    tion about China).

http://mdds.umf.maine.edu/~mshea/China/kids.html
    Books on China for kids—Bibliography of Chinese history
    and social customs for young readers

Anne Frank Online
    www.annefrank.com
    Plenty of information about Anne Frank with great resources
    and links

A Cybrary of the Holocaust
    www.remember.org
    This site is a big library of facts, interviews, links, and other
    information dealing with the Holocaust.

United States Holocaust Museum
> http://www.ushmm.org/
> This is an excellent resource.

Social Studies School Service Catalogue of Holocaust Resources
and Material
> www.socialstudies.com/holo.html
> This site is full of great teaching tools for teachers and parents.

Native American Indian Children's Books
> http://www.cynthialeitichsmith.com/nativebooks.htm
> Find books with Native American themes or characters and peruse a list of books by Native American authors.

www.TexasIndians.com
> Online site with information for children and educators and plenty of cultural information and activities.

7

Mr. Smith Goes to Washington!

I t's easy to forget or occasionally take for granted the jobs that others do in order for our lives to be better and our environment healthier. Law enforcement and the judicial system are, as always, on the front line, but others quickly follow. Those who work in the Fire Department risk their lives daily. Others work in equally important but perhaps less recognized areas such as Aviation, Public Works and Engineering, Health and Human Services, and Solid Waste Management. These people are equally committed to community safety. These are the people who labor in City Hall.

What would you do if you woke up tomorrow and discovered you couldn't drink the water, or if we had a severe shortage of water? How would the nation be affected if planes couldn't land at airports? Would it have an impact on our city? Of course it would. More and more we are interconnected.

Rather than focusing on sites, for this section we've turned our attention to some of the programs available. Many of you may not be aware of the programs for children that are offered through the mayor's office. For details call the numbers provided. Please note that sometimes the contact person has been replaced and changes may have occurred since the writing of this book.

City Hall

Becoming Exemplary Citizens of the Future!
Office of the Mayor
Houston, Texas

Mayor Lee P. Brown's Youth Programs
Contact: Ashley Johnson
Ph: 713-437-6329

To quote Mayor Brown, "As adults, it is our responsibility to culti-vate our children's lives now so they can become exemplary citizens in the future." To that end, the mayor's office sponsors four programs that are aimed at providing Houston children with a close-up look at their city government. Contact the mayor's office for more details.

Lee Brown Kids

Students are able to take advantage of an opportunity to visit with the mayor, visit council members at City Hall, and partici-pate in various educational and cultural group activities. The children receive a signed photograph of the mayor and a Lee Brown Kids T-shirt. The program occurs once a month.

Lee Brown Kids 2

The second program provides a chance for participants to see their City Hall in action. They visit City Hall and observe City Council meetings. It is hoped that the youth will gain an under-standing of why people dedicate their lives to serving their city government and their community and cultivate a sense of civic pride.

Youth Council

The Youth Council, modeled after the Houston City Council, consists of a diverse group of teenage representatives from Hous-ton's council districts. Participants get involved in city government. They talk with their peers and discuss issues affecting them and then make recommendations to Mayor Brown.

Youth Advocacy and Media Training

Teens participate in a workshop where they discuss issues of concern with the media and influence public policy. They learn to make their voices heard. They also have a chance to spur positive change in their communities and create peer-to-peer training on media literacy and public policy. This is a great opportunity to deal with two major components of our American life, the government and the media, at the same time.

Aviation Department

Contact: Gray James
Ph: 281-233-3000

Tours are 1½ - 2 hours and conducted five days a week at the request of teachers or youth program coordinators.

For children 10 years and older. Reservations required.

Youth Airports Tour Program

> **Tip:** *Additional non-airport controlled facility tours can be arranged through federal agencies, tenants, or airlines.*

Here's a current event topic. Houston's airport traffic is huge and growing every year. If you want to experience the congestion and frustration that accompanies air travel nowadays, take a trip to the airport during the Christmas holiday season. Airport traffic control and regulations are a growing concern and affect an enormous number of the city's population. Not only do children learn the civic responsibilities this department handles, but they also learn about the various jobs that are available.

The Houston Airport System sponsors a year-round Youth Airports Tour program at Bush Intercontinental Airport, Hobby Airport, and Ellington Field.

Police Department

Contact: Captain M. Fougerousse
Ph: 713-308-3200

Junior Citizens Police Academy

Here's a chance to experience firsthand the issues and situations that confront law enforcement officers daily. This 10-week course, held at the police academy, is an abbreviated version of the training that cadets go through to become officers. Police operations are explained, and it is hoped this will help bridge the gap between the department and youth by building trust, respect, and a feeling of cooperation. Junior Citizens Police Academy provides opportunities to learn firsthand what police officers do during their tour of duty. Definitely something to do if you're planning on a career in law enforcement, but still interesting if you are not.

Explorers

Law enforcement is keenly tied to civics and is certainly a potential career choice. Designed for youth ages 14 - 20 who are interested in learning about law enforcement, this year-round program explains to students what they can expect from law enforcement and the court and correction systems. Participants receive instruction in police-oriented duties and functions through the Community Services Division.

Y-PAC (Youth Police Advisory Council)

Teens who are concerned about issues affecting Houston's youth should look into this program. Y-PAC is a voluntary group of teen representatives who, as council representatives, meet at least four times a year with the police chief. They discuss current problems facing youth and how these issues relate to HPD's policies and programs. A great way for a teen to get involved and to learn civic responsibility as well as develop skills that can help her in any future work.

Police Museum

17000 Aldine-Westfield Road, Houston, Texas

Ph: 281-230-2300
Fee: Free admission
Hours: Open Monday – Friday 8 a.m. – 3:30 p.m.

Whether your children are interested in following a career in law enforcement or simply enjoying police shows on TV, all kids will be captivated by the artifacts and historical displays at the Police Museum. Interesting facts abound throughout the museum, most accompanied by an exciting display. Some thoughts to ponder:

Did you know that:

- Though the Houston Police Department (HPD) was established in 1841, there are no known artifacts from its earliest period?

- The first police officer's hat was made of cardboard and covered with a dyed mole skin?

- Sakowitz of Houston made the oldest uniform in the collection in 1915?

- Badge number "One" was first issued in 1878? No records exist as to who first wore this badge, but badge number "One" is still in service today.

- In 1912 the HPD Mounted Horse Traffic Squad was formed? These avid horsemen perform many duties including cattle roundup, traffic duty, patrol, and tracking escaped convicts.

- In 1915 officers worked 12-hour shifts and received $65 a month and maybe one day off a month?
- HPD has on display a fully restored 1952 Ford along with many artifacts and gear of the period?
- Officer Eva Jane Bacher, hired in 1918, holds the honor of first woman police officer in Houston?
- HPD Helicopter Division was established in 1970? All HPD craft markings end with the letter "F." The military alphabet uses this letter in conjunction with the word Fox. Thus, 53Fox would be the radio call numbers for the craft that now hangs in the museum.

Interactive sessions give children a chance to "ride" in a police car and check out the gun collection with the supervision of an officer.

Everyone, adults and children alike, will be interested in the exhibits of confiscated weird weapons, police uniforms from all over the world, and a police helicopter.

Municipal Courts Judicial Department

Contact: Linda Vaughn
Ph: 713-247-8746

In an era of Real TV, the Judicial Department offers its own version of reality annually in May on Law Day. (This event is open to the public.) Law Day is a good opportunity for your child to learn how and why the courts work, as well as discovering all about the judicial process from the city's own judges and lawyers. There are a variety of programs to introduce a child to the judicial process and the court systems:

- The judges can be scheduled for *Career Day* programs or speaking engagements.
- City jail and courtroom tours are available to schools by appointment.

- An annual *Law Day* is conducted during the first week of May. The department invites schools and civic organizations to participate in Law Day. Everything and anything that has to do with the municipal court system is discussed: the judge's role, the jury's role, the prosecution, and the defense. There is a mock trial so the children can observe and begin to understand what actually happens in court. Law Day is usually advertised through the papers, but you may want to call for more details.

Fire Department

Mayor's Office

Contact: Lillian Harris
Ph: 713-865-4140

Fire Station Tours

Houston has 87 fire stations, and youth groups of all ages are invited to tour any of the stations free of charge. Tours must be done during the hours of 10 a.m. – 7 p.m. and must be scheduled at least two weeks in advance, when possible.

Career Days/Special Programs

Aimed at scout troops, youth organizations, and recruiting seminars, these outreach programs provide fire safety training classes and recruiting seminars upon request.

Houston Fire Museum

Located in the historic former city fire station at 2403 Milam Street, between Gray and McGowen, just south of downtown.

Ph: 713-524-2526
Web site: www.houstonfiremuseum.org
Hours: Tuesday – Saturday, 10 a.m. – 4 p.m.
Fees: Adult $2 Children & Youth (3-17 yrs.) $1
Museum members & Seniors (65+) $1
Children under 3 Free
Group visits are encouraged but certain rules apply.

> **Tip:** *Don't miss the new "Junior Firehouse" where kids can try on bunker coats and helmets.*

Children and adults alike are welcome at the Houston Fire Museum where they state "the history of fire fighting lives on!" Your visit will not only be educational but fun and historical as well. The Houston Fire Museum preserves and displays a vast collection of artifacts relating to the history of Houston's fire service. Its mission is to educate the public about the importance of fire and life safety and the history of the fire service. The Houston Fire Department was established in 1895 with a paid crew. Now, over 100 years later, the HFD has become one of the most advanced and well-equipped services of its time.

Tips:

- No food, drinks, pets, or bicycles may be brought into the museum.
- Groups should make a reservation prior to visit.
- Individual and family memberships are available.
- Children love to climb on the museum's 1938 REO Salvage truck.
- Children's birthday parties are available.

- Safety videos are available and educational brochures from the National Fire Protection Association (NFPA) cover many aspects of fire safety and are distributed free of charge to museum patrons.

The Fire Museum encourages both public and private school tours. School children are shown a fire safety video on how to get out of a house in case of fire, and a staff member speaks about fire and life safety issues. Safety displays are set up around the room to teach children how to make a 911 call, how to check their smoke detectors, and how to locate the nearest fire station to their home, school, or parent's work.

Other Listings

Solid Waste Management Department

Dedicated to maintaining a clean, healthy environment!

Contact: Larry Stockham
Ph: 713-837-9139

This is a department that is seldom thought of, but one whose work is an integral part of our daily lives.

Storm Drain Stenciling Program
　　Here's a different way to instill civic pride in children and give them a job to do. Created to teach children about the environmental dangers of dumping chemicals and waste in the city's storm drain system, The Household Hazardous Waste section works with youth groups year round to stencil, in permanent ink, the message "You Dump It, You Drink It" or "Dump No Wastes, Drains to Bay!" These messages are stenciled on the aprons of storm drains throughout the city. The department provides the stenciling kits to youth groups.

The ReStore Westpark Consumer Recycling Center

Recycling is an important civic responsibility to instill in children. The ReStore is a new recycling and waste management education center where children can learn about recycling year round. They also have the opportunity take recycled materials and create arts and crafts. Note that the ReStore is also a book and repository swap site, as well as a repository for small items of post-consumer scrap for those interested in art projects.

Public Works and Engineering Department

Contact: Pat Truesdale
Ph: 713-837-0473

Elementary and Middle Water Conservation Education Program

Targeting grades 4-8 (presentation adjusted to age group), this program is available to schools, Girl and Boy Scout troops, Parks Department summer program groups, and other youth groups. It is the backbone of the water conservation education program. Curriculum introduces an explanation of the water and wastewater treatment processes and protection of the quality of our water supply.

"Wet in the City" Water Conservation Education Program

The "wet in the city" education program includes innovative water resource activities for students K-12. The Water Conservation Branch is a cosponsor. Water topics include water conservation, water quality, drinking water, water pollution, municipal water systems, watershed, surface and ground water, and water stewardship.

Toolbox Tips

T-shirt Design Contest and Water Conservation

For students in grades 1-8, this annual contest is part of the city's educational program to promote water conservation. Participating students create a unique T-shirt design and in doing so, contribute to the city's water conservation program while they learn about the need to conserve and manage water resources. The winner receives a trophy and T-shirt with the winning design. Contact Public Works and Engineering Department's Pat Truesdale at 713-837-0473 for details.

Arrange and Conduct Your Own Tours

Don't stop with the prepackaged tours that are available from City Hall or through various well-known facilities. Contact banks, retail stores, and/or service companies to see if they would be willing to spend a few minutes giving your child and maybe a small group of friends a behind-the-scenes tour. Newspaper companies are interesting places for kids and may be receptive to small groups.

Discover your child's interests, find out what he or she wants to be when grown. Then see if you can find someone who will show what that position entails. Not everyone has the patience to wait on the public. Not everyone is willing to be buried under a mountain of bureaucratic red tape. Getting some hands-on opportunities can help a child define his or her future place in the world.

Is your child a budding entrepreneur?

In this day and age of teen computer and financial wizards, it's possible that your child may have an entrepreneurial spirit. Newspaper carriers are no longer kids on bicycles. Times have changed, but there's still a way for your child to open some type of business.

- Plan a garage sale and put your child in charge of one area. Let her price the items, display them, and promote them. Don't forget to allow her to control the flow of money and retain some of the profits to gain experience.

- Allow your child to show fiscal responsibility. The first step in finding out where your money has gone is to track every place you spend money. Have your child track his or her spending for one full week. See if there are surprises.

- Maybe you have the next Alan Greenspan or Wall Street wizard. Have your child open an imaginary account and buy stock. Then follow the stock on the TV or in the newspaper for one to three months. Let your child determine if he made correct, informed decisions.

 Resources

Books, Brochures, and Magazine Information

FireFighters by Norman Simon (ages 2-4)

Fireman for a Day by Zilla K. McDonald

A Mice Way to Learn about Government by Peter Barnes (ages 9-12)

100 Best Careers in Crime Fighting: Law Enforcement, Criminal Justice, Private Security, and Cyberspace Crime Detection by Mary Price Lee

Every Drop Counts, a Book About Water by Jill Wheeler

Related Web Sites

The Houston Airport System
www.ci.houston.tx.us/has/
The airport system is run by the city of Houston's Department of Aviation.

www.yellowairplane.com
Kid-friendly site with pre-made model airplanes, 3D computer models, the Kids Aviation Club, and teaching your children about airplanes

The History of Aviation
cybersleuth-kids.com/sleuth/History/Aviation_History/
A complete history guide of the aviation from 1800 to today

The Kids Aviation Club
members.aol.com/MildCkn/aviation.html
Home page

Dan's Fireman Page for Kids
www2.privatei.com/~bwalko/DanFire1.htm
Fireman Dan - Age 6. Interesting fireman sites for kids

Fire Truck Video—Kids Club
www.firemanjim.com
Fireman Jim's Kids Club is great. You can sign up for membership and get a free activity book. Find puzzles and games that you can print out and solve.

www.freenet.carleton.ca/~dd385/civilnk.htm
Civics page-instructions, scavenger hunt, a really neat scrapbook, government sites, newspapers, civics quiz

Access Washington's Online Courts for Kids
access.wa.gov/kids/courts.asp
Online Courts for Kids. Learning About Law on the World Wide Web

Congressman Pombo's Web Page for Kids
   www.house.gov/pombo/kids/trivia3.htm
   U.S. Civics Quiz—This site has an online civics quiz.

Office of Water Kid's Page
   www.epa.gov/ow/kids.html
   EPA's Office of Water, Water for Kids

Drinking Water—Kids' Stuff
   http://www.epa.gov/safewater/kids/index.html
   This is a great link for kids with activities, games, and
   resources for teachers and kids.

EarthSavers: Water Conservation Tips for Kids
   www.familyeducation.com/article/0,1120,22-5860,00.html
   Did you know that every drop of water that runs down the
   drain ends up flowing into the sewage system?

8

In Your Own Backyard!

O ur main focus throughout the book has been to describe ways to make more out of a trip to museums, science centers, and other facilities. Obviously it's not always possible to load up the car and spend a day at Moody Gardens or the Museum of Natural Science, but there are activities that can be fun and still be instructive. Given a little encouragement and sometimes a helping hand, children can explore their backyard, conduct investigations in the house, and still have a good time.

The following are some ideas to get you started.

Backyard Camp-Out!

Who hasn't had a backyard camp-out? For generations children have been constructing camps in their backyards. Many families go on "real" camping trips. The fresh air and the camp experience provide an avenue for children to learn more about nature. They learn respect for nature, persistence over obstacles (have you ever tried to light a fire with sticks?), and how to interact with nature.

Cool Tips:

- Look with fresh eyes and show your excitement for the camping experience. Enthusiasm is contagious.
- If a picture is worth 1,000 words, know that showing is always better than telling. Let the child see how to tie a knot or do an experiment. Don't take over, but don't set the child adrift.
- Don't overplan; allow for spontaneity.
- In today's world even adults have a short attention span; kids have an even shorter one. Don't plan long drawn out activities.
- Have a surprise bag of treats the kids don't know about. When things lag, pull it out and offer a surprise.

- Check the child's supplies. Is everything clean from the last trip? Is the sleeping bag dry and clean?

- The children may want to camp out on their own, but they also want to know you'll be there to help out if needed. Leave when it's sleep time, but be sure to leave the back door open just in case.

- Children love to have photographs of themselves doing things. Take photos; make copies for each child.

Dylan and Kortney get ready for a backyard camp-out. © Vikk Simmons, 2001.

235

The following are activities that can be done at home or in the backyard.

Doing the ice cube lift

Stuff you'll need:

Glass of water (plastic is fine), one ice cube, some string, a dash of salt, and at least one friend.

1. Float an ice cube in a glass of water.

2. Challenge one or more friends to pick up the ice cube with the string. After they've made several attempts, show them how it's done.

3. Lay the string so the end of it is on the ice cube. Sprinkle the salt on the cube, wait a few seconds, then lift the string. The ice cube will have frozen to the string; the salt affected the freezing point of the ice.

Star Search

An all-time favorite for any camper is to search for stars and name the constellations; great fun on a clear, starry night. Did you know that the Keck Telescope located in Mauna Kea, Hawaii has a seg-mented mirror 33 feet in diameter? Talk about big and powerful.

The next exercise requires adult supervision.

Reactive Experiment

Stuff you'll need:

Quart soda bottle, cork, ½ cup water, ½ cup vinegar, 1 tsp. baking soda, paper towel, and thumbtack.

1. Pour the water and vinegar into the soda bottle.

2. Put a teaspoon of baking soda on a 4"x4" piece of paper towel.

3. Drop the paper into the bottom of the bottle and put on the cork as tightly as you can and watch what happens.

What you're observing is the pressure build-up of carbon dioxide.

Making Funny Putty

For a quieter fun activity, try making some funny putty.

Stuff you'll need:

(To extract polymers and make a kind of "goop.") White glue, borax, water, plastic film canister, covered jar, spoons, measuring cup, an adult to help.

1. Put ½ cup warm water into the jar and add a level teaspoon of borax.

2. Screw on lid and shake until dissolved.

3. In the measuring cup, add two teaspoons of water to two teaspoons of the white glue. (The measuring cup should be dry and clean when you start.)

4. Mix very well.

5. Add 1 teaspoon of your borax solution. Keep mixing and poking the blob of putty for 3 to 5 minutes. This mixing is a very important part of the process. The funny putty will be stiff and difficult to mix. Pretend it's dough and smush it like mom does when kneading the bread she bakes.

You can now stretch or mold the funny putty. Try bouncing it. If you pull slowly, the funny putty will stretch; pull quickly and "snap." Oh, and the film canister. That's to store your funny putty to keep it from drying out.

Tips:

- You'll have enough borax solution left to make more. If you don't, be sure you read the label and dispose of the solution properly.

- If you leave the funny putty in a round ball shape on a plate and come back later, it will become a shiny blob.

- Add a drop of food color while you're smushing the putty.

- Lift the ink from color comics just like the commercial stuff.

- Question to find out: If this is a polymer, what is a monomer?

Science Fun

Did you know that running water diverts light?
Here's how to prove it.

Pouring light

Stuff you'll need:
A dark room, a clear plastic bottle, water, a flashlight, and a bowl.

1. Make a hole on the bottom half of a clear plastic bottle.
2. Hold your finger over the hole and fill the bottle with water.
3. In a dark room, shine a flashlight from behind the hole and let the water pour out into the bowl. You're pouring light!

The bouncing scale

Sir Isaac Newton said that every action
has an equal but opposite reaction.

A simple way to prove it:

1. Stand on the bathroom scale with your arms raised above your head and look at your weight on the dial.
2. Now suddenly bring your arms down to your sides. The scale will show a loss in weight for an instant, then it will return to normal.
3. Try *quickly* bending your knees while standing on the scale. What happens?

Proving your "guess"

What's an "educated guess?" Here's one way to find out.

Stuff you'll need:
One glass of water, lots of paper clips.

Fill a glass to the very top with water. Guess how many paper clips you can add before the water overflows.
Try it and see!

Making a science work-kit

Experiments are fun, but sometimes it's hard
to remember where all the ingredients are stored.
Here are some suggestions for creating a handy work-kit.

Stuff you'll need:
A basket or bucket with a handle. The plastic ones used for holding cleaning supplies work well or a large tackle box.

A list of what you'll need:
Your parents or a teacher can help you with this. Try science web sites for hints; we've provided some.

Tips:

- When the experiment is finished, clean everything and put it away so it will be ready for the next experiment.

- Maintain an on-going list of things you'd like to add to the work-kit. Some items you might want to consider are: ruler, magnifying glass, small zipper locking bags for collecting, binoculars, notebook, pencils, paper clips, rubber bands, sticky notes, petri dishes, thermometer, tape measure, scotch tape, small bottle of water, disposable camera, tweezers, and small scissors.

Bubble Fun

Make great bubbles for a fraction of the cost of the
bubble solution you buy in commercial bottles.

Stuff you'll need:

Empty half-gallon milk carton, measuring cup, clear
dishwashing liquid (the more expensive name brands of soap seem
to work better for bubbles, like Dawn or Joy), glycerin (from
drugstore).

1. Rinse out the milk carton well and fill it with water. Pour out
   1/3 cup and use it to water a plant.
2. Add 1/3 cup of the dish soap and 1 tablespoon glycerin.
3. Close the carton and turn it over a couple times to mix it all
   up. Don't shake. That would make suds.

Tips:

- If you can wait, the bubbles will be better after 24 hours. If
  not, that's okay.

- Don't throw away the plastic rings from soda cans. You can
  recycle them. Use one to blow bubbles. Dip it in your bubble formula, wave, and you'll get tons of bubbles!

- *Very important:* Plastic rings from soda can six-packs are
  dangerous and terrible polluters. Birds and sea creatures
  get caught in these soda-pop can collars and may be injured
  or die. When you're done with your soda pop can collar
  bubble-blower, cut it up. Snip open all the loops or rings
  with a pair of scissors. Animals can't get trapped in the
  loops if you snip them open.

There are many items around the house that can be used for all
kinds of experiments.

Learn about crystals

What better way than to make the sweet edible kind...
Rock candy. Rock candy is just crystallized sugar.

Warning: Adult supervision is needed for this experiment. Experiment requires cooking sugars at dangerous temperatures.

Stuff you'll need:
  2 cups water, 5 cups sugar, jar, string or bamboo skewer, candy thermometer, and coffee can lid.

1. Dissolve the sugar in the water and cook until it reaches 250 degrees. This temperature is also called *hard ball*, and most cookbooks will tell you how to do it without a candy thermometer.

Important! Don't stir after you've dissolved the sugar.

2. After it's cooled a bit so it won't crack the glass, pour the hot liquid in a jar.

3. Punch a bamboo skewer through a plastic coffee can lid.

4. Lay the lid over the jar so the skewer pokes down into the middle of the liquid. Do not let the skewer touch the bottom of the jar. You can also use string. Push it through the hole in the lid and then knot it on the outside so it won't slip through the hole.

5. In 7 days, lift out the skewer and it will be covered with sugar crystals! Why did this happen? There was so much sugar dissolved, the water couldn't hold it all. Some sugar had to undissolve and grew into sugar crystals.

Green Thumb? Garden Fun!

Whether you like flowers or vegetables,
you'll really love them if you grow them yourself.

First of all, let's check the rules.

- With your parent's permission, choose the location of the garden and be sure it's all right to dig. Don't put the garden where there are buried cables. If you don't have a plot of land available, use window boxes or flower pots (see *Indoor Gardening* later in this section).

- Refer to a good gardening book or seed packet to figure out how much space is needed. Plan for a fully grown plant.

- Choose a sunny location that has good circulation, drainage, and receives rainfall.

- Draw up a Garden Plan to show how big your garden is going to be in order to contain all the plants. Leave room to walk between the rows and somewhere to put your composter.

- Keep a Garden Journal to record how and when you worked on your garden and its results.

- Note how big your garden is by multiplying the length by the width to calculate the square yardage of your plot. This will be useful later.

- Don't get too close to large trees or hedges, as they'll steal nutrients from the new plants. Put the tallest plants, like sunflowers or corn, along the back so they won't overpower shorter ones.

- Learn when to plant as well as where. Timing is important for proper growth.

Kortney holds the pot, while Dylan gets the potting soil. © Vikk Simmons, 2001.

Try Your Hand at Indoor Gardening

So what if it's raining! You can still plant. Start your garden with seedlings. Some fruits and vegetables like cantaloupe, cucumbers, squash, and watermelon should be started in individual containers and transplanted without disturbing the roots.

To start seeds indoors:

Stuff you'll need:

A sunny window or a place under cool white flourescent bulbs, several containers. (clean with good drainage), seeds, growing medium that provides sterile soil free of unwanted weed seeds. You can make your own from many good recipes on web sites or in gardening books.

1. Fill pots to within ¼ inch of the top with your potting mixture and level the surface.

2. Water the soil and allow it to drain thoroughly first.

3. Make a hole for each seed with a pencil or chopstick. Most seeds need to be planted four times as deep as the seed is wide, but if your seeds are very fine, cover them with a fine layer of soil.

4. Keep your new plantings evenly moist but not soaking wet. Too much moisture will rot the seeds. A fine sprayer works best, or water from the bottom.

Tips:

- Plastic African violet pots work well and can be found in a tiny size at the supermarkets, but you may have to request them if they're out of season.

- Slip your pots into plastic bags to keep the humidity and moisture even and reduce the frequency of watering.

- Some seeds require light to germinate while others prefer total darkness. The seed packet lists requirements. Once germinated, all seedlings need light to develop. Supplement the natural light with flourescent bulbs if necessary.

- Watch your plantings carefully as this is a critical time for seedlings.

- Small pots dry out quickly, so check them often. If your seedlings are growing in a windowsill, turn them often so the stems will grow straight.

- The first two leaves you will see on the plant are not true leaves but food storage cells called *cotyledons*. Once the first true leaves have developed, fertilizing begins. A weak solution of a good liquid organic fertilizer works well.

- One week before transplanting your seedlings outdoors, you need to "harden them off" (prepare them for the outside). Move the plants to a shady outdoor area at first, but bring them indoors for the night if the night temperatures drop. Each day, move them out into the sun for a few hours, increasing the time spent in the sun. Keep them well watered during this period, and don't place them directly on the ground if slugs are a problem. Monitor closely for insect damage.

- Don't be in a hurry to transplant. When you are ready, thoroughly water the seedlings and the ground outside before transplanting. Transplant on a cloudy day so strong sun won't wilt your seedlings.

- Dig a hole about twice the size of the root ball and set the transplant into the hole so the root ball will be covered by ¼ inch of soil. Press the soil firmly around the roots. A small depression around the plant stem will help trap moisture. Water immediately and deeply for the first week so the plants won't develop shallow roots.

> *Centipede walking*
> *Faster and faster it moves*
> *Going, going, gone.*

—Mandi Coppock, age 10

Creepy, Crawly Things

Spiders spinning webs
Flies getting deceived by weaves
Now the fly is lunch

—Mandi Coppock, age 10

Did you know:

- Bugs can be beautiful as well as beneficial; others can be pesky? What's a good "pollution solution"? Instead of using pesticides, the Chinese use thousands of ducks that eat about 200 insects every hour.

- If you live in Texas, you know about cockroaches. But did you know they can live up to 9 days without a head?

- Guess the number of insects and spiders in a jar that add up to 10 and that have a total of 68 legs. How many of each are there? Give up? (6 insects and 4 spiders)

- Do you know what entomology is? Entomology is the study of insects, and the people who study them are called entomologists.

If you'd like to do a little insect studying yourself, pick a project like this one:

Let's build an Ant Habitat!

Like bees, wasps, and termites, ants live in groups called colonies and are very social. An ant habitat is a good way to observe their behavior.

> **Note:** You don't have to house train these "pets." The ants will be low-maintenance pets that will show your child more about the world of insects.

Dylan, age 8, entranced by a still butterfly. © Vikk Simmons, 2000.

Stuff you'll need:

A large glass jar, soft drink can, black construction paper, tape, sand, dirt, and ants from an ant hill, a piece of sponge, food scraps.

1. Fill the soft drink can with sand.
2. Seal the opening with tape or use an unopened can of soda.
3. Put the can into the glass jar.

4. Next, fill the rest of the glass jar with dirt and ants. Do not pack the dirt too tightly, but fill the entire jar. The ants won't be able to enter the can, so they'll build tunnels around it near the outside of the jar where you can see them.

5. Place a wet piece of sponge on top of the soft drink can, and be sure to keep it moist.

> *Important:* Cover the jar with a piece of cloth secured with a rubber band so the ants cannot crawl out.

The black paper taped around the outside of the jar will force the ants to tunnel against the dark sides of the jar.

It may be a week or so before the tunnel complex begins developing, but you can remove the paper for short periods to observe the ants' behavior.

> *Important:* You must feed the ants. Place food scraps on top of the dirt. When you observe them feeding, you can tell what food they like best. Try offering sugar water, dry pet food, and pieces of fruit.

> *Tip: Keep notes on their behavior.*

Insects indoors and outdoors when it's cold

Insects are everywhere, even in winter, though they may seem scarce. Don't be fooled into thinking they're gone. Insects go into *overwintering*; that's how an insect survives the winter months.

Most insects do not like the cold and will try to keep warm when temperatures drop. To survive, some will lay eggs that will hatch when it's warmer, and some migrate to warmer places. Some insects even sleep through the winter. They are called *dormant*.

Exercise

● How about searching for some dormant insects? Check out old tree stumps, rotten bark, under fallen leaves, right under the ground you walk on. You could find eggs, larvae, pupae, or adult insects overwintering.

- Next, try the house. Look in corners, houseplants, and stacks of old newspapers, recycling bins, piles of firewood, and cabinets. (You may have a new roommate.)

- You might find a house or cobweb spider. Usually these arthropods hide in corners and spin irregular webs, not graceful, beautiful ones like some other spiders, to catch any flies, moths, or mosquitoes that have made your house their home.

To watch a spider

- Place a cobweb spider in a terrarium or jar. The spider will spin a web. Add a fly or small moth to the jar. When the insect flies into the web, the spider will race over and grab its victim. The spider will wrap silk around the insect so it can't escape. The housefly, found everywhere, is a good source of food for the spider. The housefly has one of the shortest life cycles in the insect world: Its entire life lasts between six and twenty days. It can perform one interesting feat: It can walk on ceilings without falling.

- Another fly you might find around the house is the pomace fly or fruit fly. They develop rapidly and can produce almost 25 generations a year. Each female fruit fly lays up to 100 eggs, half of which will hatch into males and half into females.

- One of the few insects covered with scales, silverfish, are also found in the home. This silvery or gray insect prefers damp places and loves to chomp on book bindings, papers, cards, and boxes—all meals for the silverfish.

Some other insects that overwinter are earwigs, cockroaches, and ants.

- Earwigs overwinter as either eggs or adults. Earwigs do not bite but if handled, might pinch.

- During winter or any time of the year the hearty cockroaches, those brown, shiny, flat-bodied creatures, might be found skittering around the house. It's almost impossible to eliminate them. After all they have been around for 350 million years. In those days they were at least 6 inches long!

If you find an unwanted winter visitor, just help it along to its natural overwintering stage; catch it carefully in a jar and release it outside.

Collect insects from the lawn/make a net

- Collect insects outside by using a method known as sweeping. Sweeping involves swinging an insect net back and forth like sweeping a floor with a broom.
- Make an inexpensive insect net constructed from a wire coat hanger.

1. Bend the hanger into a square.
2. The bag for the net should be made from a fine mesh fabric. A five-gallon nylon paint strainer is perfect. Inexpensive strainers can be found at most paint stores.
3. The wire hanger can be connected to a broom handle or 36-inch wooden dowel with duct tape. Most home supply stores have inexpensive dowels.
4. Use an insect field guide to identify the insects you find. Simon & Schuster's *Guide to Insects* by Ross H. Arnett Jr. and Richard L. Jaques Jr. is easy to read.
5. Sweep the net by swinging it back and forth so that a flat side is brushing the tops of the blades of grass for about 30 seconds.
6. Swing the net quickly through the air to force the insects to the bottom. Grab the net about one-third of the way up from the bottom to keep the insects from escaping. Have a friend hold a clear, zipper lock type bag, then turn the insect net

inside out into the bag and shake. Once the insects are inside, seal the bag.

7. Release the insects outside after you have made your observations

Answer these questions in your nature journal:

Count the number and kinds of insects. Try to identify as many insects as you can. How many different colors of insect are there in the bag? Do you think an insect's color might help keep it from being eaten by other animals? What else did you catch besides insects? Do the same thing for 60 seconds. In the 60-second collections did you catch more insects than in the 30-second collections?

Tip: When sweeping, be careful to avoid areas of the lawn with clover or other flowers to avoid catching bees and getting stung.

And speaking of spiders

Did you ever wonder why spiders don't get caught in their own webs? Here's an experiment that will help you to understand.

Stuff you'll need:

Clear tape like Scotch brand tape, cooking oil.

1. Place a piece of tape on a table with the sticky side up.

2. Pretend you're a bug and walk with your fingers across the tape.

3. Put another piece of tape on the table.

4. Dip your fingers in the cooking oil and walk across the tape again. What happened?

The reason spiders don't usually get caught in a web is they're careful where and how they place their feet, and the tips of their feet are oily. Another interesting fact is that not all spiders use silken webs to trap insects. Some spiders jump and pounce. Others run.

How to go webbing

Important! This should be done with adult supervision.

Stuff you'll need:

Heavy paper, water-based spray paint

1. Some spiders are dangerous. Remember you are looking for webs, not spiders.
2. Search the yard, all corners of your house, or a park.
3. *Important!* Make sure there isn't a spider nearby.
4. Once you find a web, spray it with the paint. Do this gently so the spray doesn't break the web.
5. Put the paper behind the web.
6. Lift the paper until the support silk breaks.

The web will stay on the paper. The paint will stick the web down and make it visible.

> **Fact:** Spider silk is stronger than the same weight of steel. But the real reason spider silk is so special is it can stretch very far without breaking, which is the secret of its strength.

Backyard Habitat

A backyard is filled with wonderful sights, such as butterflies and hummingbirds.

How do you say butterfly in some other languages?

Here's just a few:

Malaysian *rama-rama*	Chinese *hu die*
French *papillon*	Hebrew *parpar*
Hopi Native American *masivie* (PG)	
Italian *farfalla*	Kikuyu *kihuruta* (PG)
Polish *motyl*	Spanish *mariposa*
Welsh *gloyn byw*	

And in sign language: *interlocked thumbs, flapping hands like wings.*

Fact: Adult butterflies, as well as caterpillars, breathe through a series of tiny openings along the sides of their bodies, called *spiracles*. From each spiracle, a tube called a *trachea* carries oxygen into the body. Butterflies don't have noses and lungs as we do; they "smell" with their antennae.

Dylan and Kortney fill the bird feeders. © Vikk Simmons, 2001.

Ever wonder where a butterfly comes from? It comes from a chrysalis (KRIS-uh-liss), which is also called a pupa. A chrysalis looks like a tiny leathery pouch. You can find one underneath some leaves in the summer.

If you want to see lots of butterflies around your yard this summer, you need a fondness for caterpillars. A butterfly garden is a wonderful way to watch butterflies.

Making a butterfly garden is simple and fun. Plant native prairie wildflowers, the kind of plants butterflies like. Zinnias are a natural for the butterfly garden, attracting many butterflies through their long blooming season. Phlox provide a sweet and colorful garden treat for butterflies, moths, and bumblebees; over 60 species are available for spring or summer, sun or shade.

Some other butterfly plants: ageratum, bee balm, bougainvillea, calendula, coneflower, dahlia, daylily, geranium, hibiscus, impatiens, marigold, milkweed, mint family, salvia, snapdragon, yarrow, yellow sage.

Remember, the best plants for a butterfly garden are those that flower for a long period of time, are fragrant, grow in colorful clumps, and have large petals or blossoms that provide easy access to the nectar butterflies eat.

> **Tip:** *Sunlight is an important ingredient for a butterfly garden. Butterflies are cold-blooded, so the sun helps them stay warm.*

Butterfly Quiz

- Which species of flowers attract the most butterflies?
- Do the butterflies prefer one color to another?
- What time of day did you see the most butterflies?
- Does the butterfly flap its wings while feeding?
- How many other insects did you see enjoying the garden picnic?

To Attract Birds

To attract birds to your garden you need to provide a good environment. Birds require plants for food, nesting, and protection. Birds also require fresh clean water. With the right plants and the proper environment, you can turn part of your yard, or even a small patio, into a butterfly magnet and/or bird sanctuary.

The hummingbird is a special bird because it's so different and so much fun to watch. Why not watch a hummingbird up close? You could see it fly backward and sideways and hover like a helicopter! Plant red tube-shaped flowers if you want them to visit. Bee balm is a good plant, *Monarda Cambridge Scarlet*. Other plants include trumpet-creeper, trumpet honeysuckle, fire pink, cardinal flower, red buckeye, scarlet penstemon, coral bells, cypress vine, scarlet bush, scarlet paintbrush, geiger tree, scarlet salvia, scarlet petunia, and scarlet morning glory

Making a hummingbird feeder

Hang a hummingbird feeder in your backyard. You can make a feeder with a small jar that has a narrow neck, or you can use a small milk carton with holes punched in its sides. Since hummingbirds like bright colors, put red ribbons, red paper, or red tape around the eating holes to attract them. Use wire to hang your feeders. Don't forget to keep them filled.

Nectar recipe for hummingbirds

Stir ¼ cup of white sugar into one cup of boiling water. Do not substitute honey for the sugar because a honey mixture may cause disease in the birds. Do not use artificial sweeteners as there is no nutritional value in them and may cause starvation. Your feeder should be cleaned every three to five days, using a brush and detergent. Be sure to rinse it well!

Fun Facts

- How long will the footprints left on the moon by the Apollo astronauts last? They will be there for over 10 million years.

- If you placed all of the blood vessels in the human body end to end, they would extend almost 60,000 miles.

- Do you know the name of our galaxy? Hint: it's a popular candy bar. The Milky Way. What are the nine planets in our solar system?

- Comets have tails because the solar winds from the sun blow the comet's gas and dust away, creating two tails. The Great Comet of 1843 had a tail about 220 million miles long. If the tail wrapped around Earth, it would circle the equator about 8,000 times.

- If all the ice on Earth melted, the oceans would rise about 20 feet and many major cities such as Tokyo, New York, and London would be underwater.

- How hot is a bolt of lightning? 50,000 degrees F. or five times hotter than the sun's surface. Whew!

- The universe contains more stars than all the grains of sand on all the beaches of the world.

- Scientists have discovered seeds over 10,000 years old, which could still grow.

- The bamboo plant in Asia can grow up to 36 inches in one day.

- Which animal living today has the largest eyes? Would you believe it's the squid?

- The rainforest is said to be disappearing at about 40,000 miles or more per year.

- Some medicines are made from rainforest trees. Aspirin and quinine come from trees, and cough medicine can be made from a tree resin.

Resources

Books

The Everything Kids' Nature Book by Kathiann M. Kowalski. "Kids love nature, and with *The Everything Kids' Nature Book*, they'll keep busy for hours. Packed with information and activities, kids will roam the natural world of their own backyard. Discover how birds, bats, and bugs pollinate the landscape. Learn about life on the edge of the sea and more!"

Butterflies & Moths by Bobbie Kalman & Tammy Everts. Good photos of moths and butterflies. Fun facts such as what they eat, how they are different from each other, and what the colors on their wings mean are also revealed.

Butterflies Glow-in-the-Dark Sticker Book From monarchs to purple emperors to plate-sized Hercules moths, everything anyone wants to know about the fluttering, colorful world of butterflies in a new sticker book. With the eye-catching glow-in-the-dark stickers, kids can create a luminescent butterfly sanctuary world of their own. 16 pages + 2 sticker pages. Ages 6 and up.

Golden Guide to Bats of the World A handsomely illustrated guide about the natural history of bats including identifying features, flight abilities, habitats, and behavior.

Bats for Kids Full of fascinating bat facts. Learn about what bats eat and how they locate their food, where they live, and the valuable role they play in nature. Color photos and illustrations. Ages 8-12.

Extremely Weird Birds by Sarah Lovett. An introduction to birds for young readers, with numerous photos and drawings; ABA Children's "Pick of the List"; YALSA Recommended Books for Reluctant Young Adult Readers; Benjamin Franklin Award.

Stars and Planets by Alastair Smith

Web Sites

http://home.earthlink.net/~stcarr/science_education.html
Kids can find out about anything and everything.

http://www.ecomall.com/biz/kidslinks.htm
Kids and ecology—teaching green

http://butterflyweb site.com/educate/index.cfm
About butterflies

http://www.the-garden-gnome.com/kids/
A gardening page for children with educational projects and experiments, a Gnome Friends bulletin board for children to display their artistic and literary endeavors about gnomes, gardening, and nature in general, topics of interest for children's research

http://www.uky.edu/Agriculture/Entomology/ythfacts/bugfun/bugfun.htm
Crafts, projects, and fun with bugs

Science Made Simple
http://www.sciencemadesimple.com
Science for kids—"Children's science experiments, simple science projects & kids science questions answered by *Science Made Simple*. Kids learn science the easy, hands-on way with *Science Made Simple*. Get fun science projects & great experiments using household materials. Clear, detailed answers to children's science questions." —*Science News*

http://www.hhmi.org/coolscience
Dive into a miniature world—without a microscope…cool science for curious kids

http://www.halcyon.com/sciclub/kidproj1.html
Kid's science projects; quick and easy experiments and short demonstrations

The National Gardening Association/ Kidsgardening
   http://store.yahoo.com/nationalgardening/
   Lots of environment through hands-on activities that make
   learning fun. Welcome to our Kidsgardening.com store. Check
   out the teacher's resource room. E-mail newsletter.

http://www.eskimo.com/fwc
   List of over 350 kid's science books

It's Our Kids' Nature
   http://www.fwconserv.org/kid's_hills.htm
   Kids and nature. "On this page we hope to build links to examples of this theme, at home and around the world."

http://kidscience.miningco.com
   About science and nature for kids

http://www.kidsastronom.com/
   Astronomy and space for kids. Ask an expert and see the sky
   tonight in real time!

Kids Earth and Sky, Connect the Stars
   http://earthsky.com/Kids/Connect-Stars/
   "You've probably played connect-the-dots before. But you've
   probably never played 'connect-the-stars.' Print out these cool
   pictures of constellations and draw lines between the stars!
   You can also color in the legendary characters that ancient
   skywatchers saw in the stars—like bears, warriors, snakes, and
   fish!"

http://www.surfnetkids.com/creepy.htm
   Best bug site for kids. "Why do kids love bugs? I don't know,
   but parents seem to fall into two camps: those that tolerate
   bugs for science's sake and those that don't. The latter are
   always apologetic. They know bugs are a part of nature and
   they know their kids love bugs. Whether you're a bug tolerator
   or not, treat your kids to these creepy creatures. They will
   thank you for it!"

http://members.aol.com/YESedu/kidsfun.html
   Kids, bugs, and fun; all about insects

The Magic School Bus explores Bugs
   http://www.microsoft.com/kids/msb/bugs.htm
   Each terrarium created by the students in Ms. Frizzle's™ class
   is missing one of its bugs! Shrink down to wee-bug size and
   help find the missing bugs with *Scholastic's The Magic School
   Bus*®!

http://www.gorp.com/gorp/publishers/foghorn/camp_kid.htm:
20%camping
   Outdoors with kids

9

Where Fun is the only Game in Town!

Although a case can be made for educational opportunities at amusement parks—consider the matter of physics applied to roller coasters—there are times when your child simply wants to run free. The following is a short list of several major amusement parks in the Houston area.

The Kemah Boardwalk

A Vacation on the Water
Located near State Highway 146 and the Clear Creek Channel

"Kemah" is a Karankawa Indian word meaning "wind in the face." This accurately depicts the Kemah Boardwalk experience with its sea breeze. This is the ideal family destination with restaurants, hotels, and a dancing fountain flanked by Galveston Bay and the Lafayette Landing Marina, but the amusement rides are the focus for kids. Rides include a carousel, a Ferris wheel, Crazy Sub, and a train.

- *Ferris wheel*—A 65-foot Century Ferris wheel with safe gondola seating for a highly different view of the boardwalk.

- *Gas powered train*—A replica of an 1863 Central Pacific Railroad train named the *C.P. Huntington* that tours the boardwalk while its conductor regales the kids with stories of Kemah's history and the waterfront.

- *Carousel*—A classic carousel with elaborate animal figures whirling to the sounds of music with delighted children on board.

Jungle Surf Water Park

Affordable Family Entertainment!
94th & Seawall, Galveston, Texas

Ph: 409-744-4737
Fees: Call for admission prices; season passes available.
Hours: Open 10 a.m. daily, spring through fall
Full snack bar

Lots of water play here with a super long-run slide, a new water tag game, kiddie pool and slide, play center, and even more slides. Parents will enjoy the shaded seating areas. Call for details on birthday parties, company events, and private outings.

Six Flags AstroWorld Houston

901 Kirby Drive, Houston, Texas 77054

Ph: 713-799-1234
Web site: www.sixflags.com
Fees: Call for admission prices; season passes available.
Hours: Open daily during the summer
Open during spring break and weekends (check for dates)

Is your idea of fun where you jump onto a roller coaster and ride through a series of spirals, high-speed drops, and hairpin turns? Like to feel your hands and legs dangle in the air? Then the new Serial Thriller roller coaster is for you. This ride takes you to the outer limits on the only suspended looping roller coaster in Texas. Speed along at up to 55 mph, climb 102 feet, plummet 10 stories, and blast through three twists, two loops, and two spins. That's only one of a multitude of experiences awaiting you and your child.

263

Texas Tornado. Photo courtesy of Six Flags AstroWorld.

Six Flags WaterWorld

901 Kirby Drive, Houston, Texas 77054

Ph: 713-799-1234
Web site: www.sixflags.com
Hours: Open daily during the summer.
Fees: Call or go to the web site for current admission prices and
hours.

Two new attractions were added in 2000: Big Kahuna, a family raft
ride; and Hook's Lagoon, a multilevel interactive treehouse.

Enron Field

Located in downtown Houston at Union Station
501 Crawford, Suite 400
Houston Astros, P.O. Box 288, Houston, Texas 77001

Ph: 713-259-TOUR (8687)
Web site: www.astros.com
Walk-Up Tour Prices:
    Adults $7   Seniors 65+ $5   Children to 14 $3
Group Reservation Prices (25 or more):
    The private, reserved group tours, groups of 25 or more,
    must make reservations at least two weeks in advance and
    are first come, first served.
Tour Enron Field:
    Adults $5   Seniors 65+ $3   Children to 14 $2

Enron Field stands and seating. © Elaine L. Galit, 2000.

Sit in the dugout where Jeff Bagwell sits! Tours leave every two hours and last approximately one hour. The tour covers one mile, so wear comfortable shoes. All tours are wheelchair accessible. Tours are scheduled during baseball season and are held at specified times.

Once more Houston is proud to have an architectural jewel in the new innovative stadium. A vintage, full-sized locomotive runs along 800 feet of track on the left-field wall and reflects the historical relationship Houston has had with the railroad. Enron Field has a retractable roof, and the building exterior is red brick masonry and natural glass. The tour includes Historic Union Station, luxury suites, club level, press box, the field, and more.

Education programs, Kindergarten - 8th Grade

Take advantage of the low cost and educational experience for students. The group will spend time in the Learning Center. The teachers receive a curriculum packet, and the groups receive a two-day subscription to the *Houston Chronicle*. Tours for children include 25 minutes in the Learning Center, an interactive area where baseball becomes a teaching tool.

Enron Field mural on inside wall (Artist: Denise Tieken). © Elaine L. Galit, 2000.

About the Authors

The authors are always happy to hear about your experiences exploring Houston or your suggestions for future volumes. We are also available for speaking engagements. Contact information is listed below, including e-mail addresses, or visit our web site at

exploringhoustonwithchildren.com

Elaine L. Galit is an award-winning freelance writer with over 100 articles and stories published. Her articles and photograph credits include *Writer's Digest, Cowboy Sports and Entertainment, Houston Maturity Magazine, Woman's World,* and on the web at NeighborhoodAmerica.com. Elaine is a member of Houston Writers Council, Romance Writers of America, and Houston Writers League. She has taught writing workshops for both adults and juniors as well as writing classes at the University of Houston, Cinco Ranch. Elaine lives in Houston, Texas with her calico cat, Juni.

Elaine Galit
14354 Memorial Drive
PMB 1067
Houston, Texas 77079
e-mail: EHWC123@AOL.com

Vikk Simmons received an MFA in Creative Writing from Vermont College and has won awards for her novel-length fiction. Her articles on writing have appeared in magazines and newsletters across the country. She is a certified journal writing instructor and conducts journal writing workshops as well as interactive writing workshops such as Fast Fiction, Writing with Passion, and Exploring an Urban Jungle. Her experience includes four years coordinating book events and promotions. She has spoken at conferences, workshops, and meetings on the business and craft of writing. Vikk appeared in *The Power of the Pen*, a TV feature story on the benefits of journal writing. She lives in northwest Houston.

Vikk Simmons
P.O. Box 430577
Houston, Texas 77243
e-mail: VikkSimmons@AOL.com

Index